No Murderers Please!
*The 18 Types Of Men To Avoid
In Online Dating
If You're Looking For Mr. Right
Or Even Just Mr. Decent.*

By: Stevie Striker

No Murderers Please!
Waxwing Publishing
POB 958, Marana, AZ, 85653 U.S.A

Copyright © 2016 Waxwing Publishing
ISBN-13: 978-1535401661
ISBN-10:   1535401664

All rights reserved. Except for brief excerpts for review purposes, no parts of this book may be reproduced or used in any form without written permission from the publishers.

Cover design by Spot On
Printed in the U.S.A

This book is dedicated to my daughter,
Meester Meister Moe,
but she's not allowed to read it until 2022.

Introduction

Recently, in the 'Viagra triangle,' a shopping and dining area in Chicago, known for its aging but fighting it all the way clientele, a man who I met online sat beside me in a restaurant on our first date and decided it would be a good idea to stick his hand into the back of my pants. Fortunately, I am long gone but, unfortunately, this human oddity will undoubtedly be sticking his hands down another uninterested woman's pants in public while calling her uptight when she protests.

That experience and many others that I've been subjected to since starting online dating have compelled me to write The Red Flag Series. I've been inspired by the pure idiocy and cluelessness of men I've met, to share my experiences and thoughts in hopes that I can help you along in the process of using online dating sites to your highest end. Women really could be laughing rather than crying over the basic fact that many of the men we meet through online sites are going to be weird. Is this because the online dating pool is a snapshot of the general male population or because online dating attracts odd birds? We may never know. The irony is that the same sites and apps that can bring us any creeper whose mother has a computer in her basement might also introduce us to a new interesting friend or something more to add to our lives.

The Red Flag Series is not about how to find or attract the perfect man or how to change so that he will fall in love with you. I am already assuming that you're pretty darn great; that you know who you are and how you feel and what you want. The Red Flag Series is meant to give you a little help in the area of online dating. Believe me, it is a different world than what most of us inhabit. I hope to help you navigate through the monumental task of weeding out the undesirables. If you want to be productive, this approach can be much more useful and efficient than worrying about whether you are giving men enough of a chance or being too hard on them. And unlike many other books on dating for women, these manuals are not written to describe to you how to be more feminine and attractive to men. They are not written to help you learn how to compromise who you are by behaving differently or hiding your true feelings so that you can attract or secure some clueless or careless man who ultimately isn't a good match for you.

Humans are complex creatures. It's difficult to slot people into categories and have them fit perfectly but it can help to mentally place a man into a category of sorts. The skill is to assess him quickly and make decisions based not only on intuition but also on signals that he sends consciously and unconsciously. The Red Flag Series will help you better read and understand the online dating world. The categories or 'types' in this book are based on real people. Many I have known personally.

Others I have discovered through countless hours of talking with women who are in the online trenches and through studying psychological literature. Some may feel this series is written by a man hater, but this is far from the truth. It's written from a place of wanting to aid the perpetuation of the human species in a positive direction by helping women avoid relationships with negative men. This leaves their time and hearts open to those insightful, strong and mature men that will appreciate and cherish a strong feminine presence in their lives. This series has been in the making for most of my adult life. I hope it makes you laugh and maybe even sharpens the blurry lines a bit for you.

Table of Contents

Chapter 1
   The Massage Guy   1

Chapter 2
   Spoiled Rich Guy   5

Chapter 3
   The "Separated" or Still Married Guy   10

Chapter 4
   The Puppet Master   13

Chapter 5
   The Mentally Deranged Loose Cannon   21

Chapter 6
   The High Mach   24

Chapter 7
   The Wolf in Sheep's Clothing   29

Chapter 8
   Megalomaniacal Master of the Universe   39

Chapter 9
   Pining Man   49

Chapter 10
   The Peacock: Is He Really Just Metro?   53

Chapter 11
   Whisky Dick   64

Chapter 12
   Middle Age Mr. Perfect   69

Chapter 13
   The Clueless Clown - AKA - "You Think You Have a Chance with Me?" Guy   75

Chapter 14
   Mr. You're OK, I'm Not OK   80

Chapter 15
   The Buzz Kill   84

Chapter 16
   The Playa   92

Chapter 17
   The Not Funny Guy   96

Chapter 18
   The Piker   99

Acknowledgements   103

Bibliography   105

Chapter 1

The Massage Guy

I'm all for massages. They are spectacular. But the Massage Guy takes a beautiful thing and serves it up cold and cheesy. PDA abounds with this ladies' man. He is spoiled and rotten. And you can bet he has gotten away with it before. Don't be another woman who gives in to an entitled bully. We need to train wayward guys to behave like gentlemen so the next woman doesn't have to suffer the same fate. The Massage Guy might be hard to spot if you are sitting across from him, far out of reach at a meal or for a drink.

At first meeting he will probably be careful not to start his moves right away. He will give you a hug when he first meets you and possibly try to kiss your cheek. His goal for you and for the beginning of the night is to get a reading on your receptiveness to being physical with him. Watch to see if he's trying to get you to drink more. He may also be priming himself by over drinking to get up the nerve to be obnoxious. Usually, a man like this will be a charming enough guy. He uses charm to play off his inappropriate touching as if it's funny or normal. He might try to hold your hand numerous times even if you say it's making you uncomfortable. But most go right into the age old "creepy, uncomfortable back massage from a desperate stranger" moves. Once he's got

No Murderers Please!

you in place he will go through all or most of these Red Flags.

Massage Guy's Red Flag Checklist:

- ☐ He suggests you meet at the bar. This way he can position himself correctly to touch you when he feels like he deserves it and the time is right.
- ☐ If you are seated too far away from him for a meal, he will suggest you sit at the bar for an after dinner drink.
- ☐ He will have a speech about how he's into massage and how he's studied it in books, workshops or school. He will act as if it's not sexual. Here he wants to make it seem like he's really just like a physical therapist comping you a massage.
- ☐ He will probably just go for the shoulders first. This is a ballsier move and most of these guys are supremely arrogant.
- ☐ He will mention how tight you are.
- ☐ If he's a jock, he will act like he's doing you the favor of some deep tissue massage. You need it, based on his professional opinion.
- ☐ When you get embarrassed or uncomfortable because he is doing this in public and because you just met the jerk, he will either laugh off your

The Massage Guy

protests or move to the arm that's closest to him to seem less creepy and desperate. Chances of him taking his hands off of you completely are slim, unless you get visibly angry and you may not want to do this for various reasons.

- ☐ He may try to kiss you somewhere on your body during this whole process, cheek, hand, shoulder, etc.
- ☐ When you protest that you would rather he didn't do it, his next move will be to tell you that you are being dramatic, uptight, high strung or something therein. This name calling is, of course, a manipulation to get you to think that it's normal for a man to be massaging a woman he just met, in public, against her will.

Some may even put their hand on your back and migrate into your pants. Believe me, it happens. The best way to handle The Massage Guy is to exit the situation as soon as possible. Don't explain your reason for leaving. It will be a waste of your breath. He won't comprehend anything you say anyhow. He is in denial that he's a socially challenged creep and will justify his behavior by knowing in his own mind that you are uptight (see Overt Narcissist and Control Freak coming up for more information).

No Murderers Please!

My daddy always told me, "When you step in dog shit do you sit and look at it, dig through it with a popsicle stick trying to figure out what it is? No! You wipe it off your shoe and move on". This man is just dog shit. There's nothing there to figure out.— Dawn Faulkner

Chapter 2

Spoiled Rich Guy

None of us want to date an unemployed bum. A guy with some bucks in the bank is always a plus, but what comes with a man who's got money isn't always pretty. To begin with, the more successful man generally has more power, with power comes confidence, with increased confidence comes his confidence in the ability to attract women. In addition to this confidence he may also have other women who are pursuing him quite aggressively. A 2011 study in the Journal Psychological Science found a positive relationship with infidelity and power. The higher the income, the more apt he is to cheat. Now, if that's not enough fun for you, he's got plenty more in store.

Spoiled Rich Guy may be fairly easy to spot in his profile depending on the app or site. He will probably show himself in a Ferrari or standing next to some other expensive road, air or water vehicle in one of his photos. Another shot may be with his feet up on a beautiful wooden desk making a presumably important call or standing on a stage giving a world changing speech.

The profile of the Spoiled Rich Guy will not subtly hint that he's is successful or wealthy. He may add how "thankful for it" he is, to give the impression that he's got humility on his side. But a guy like this is anything but.

No Murderers Please!

He knows that his success is all his own doing. It has nothing to do with luck, help from others or the life he was born into. Spoiled Rich Guy may call himself an Entrepreneur, Founder, Dr., CEO, CFO, or Philanthropist with his main hobbies being giving money to charities or poker tables. He may show half-photos of himself on exotic vacations with other women cropped out, just so you know he's desirable. He will also show himself doing his expensive hobbies, motor gliding, equestrian sports or traveling the world to scuba dive or climb mountains.

Of course, he won't tell you just yet about his other hobbies which can include: exploiting women, whining, cheating, being utterly deserving of privileges and demanding special treatment. He will mention that he's got the means and all he needs is someone to share it with, his partner in white-collar crime.

If he makes it through your initial screening without coming across as spoiled, don't worry. He will make up for it in spades once you spend some time with him. He may start by sending you texts or emails introducing himself with a generic compliment thrown your way. He then moves into, "Let me tell you a little bit about myself." This isn't just him making you an unusually kind offer. It goes deeper than that. (See also Megalomaniacal Master of the Universe).

If you do end up on a date with this creep, you're going to regret it. This isn't just a guy who has some money. This one is entitled to whatever he desires, in the moment and out. He's going to do things on your date and want things from you that many other men wouldn't even consider but may have dreamed about.

The Spoiled Rich Guy Red Flags:

- ☐ **Too personal** - Asks very personal questions that are none of his business.
- ☐ **One upper** – He'll One Up you in anything and everything.
- ☐ **Allows you a glimpse of his brilliance** - Talks about how he makes his millions.
- ☐ **Lifestyles of the rich and famous** - Talks about what he does with his money and while doing this will show you how deeply special he is. Here he may drop a few names.
- ☐ **PDA** - Tries to touch you in ways that give you the creeps.
- ☐ **Insults** - Uses insults before and after he doesn't get his way.
- ☐ **Overly critical and rude** - He will probably be judgmental and rude to you either knowingly or unknowingly.
- ☐ **You're lucky to be with him** - May look down his nose at you as he leans back in his chair

with his legs spread towards you so you can get a really good look.

- ☐ **Overly educated prick** – He's had the best in life from the beginning including elite education, trips across the globe, endless toys and other privileges that came from being born into them. This doesn't always make a man spoiled but it's more likely that he's going to look down on you if he is more educated, wealthier and worldly than you are. This type of spoiled man would call hanging out with you "slumming it."
- ☐ **Expects handouts** - He's used to having people fawn over him and give him things for free. Because of this, he doesn't like to work for anything, you included. He is that guy you take to a dinner or BBQ at your friend's home who brings nothing and is the only one who leaves with leftovers.

Just because he has money doesn't mean he's intelligent, classy, or has well-developed social skills. Spoiled Rich Guy has no doubt gotten much of what he's wanted from countless females in his past. He is also more likely to be surrounded in his life by 'yes men'. He has probably gotten away with a lot of questionable things and who knows, maybe even murder. If at any point when you're describing your date with him to your friend and you hear her say in a bewildered tone, "Who does that?" or "Who thinks like that?" or even "What an ass clown!" you know your screening process wasn't thorough enough. Leave the money and run.

There is less in this than meets the eye. —Tallulah Bankhead

For the modern girl, opportunity doesn't knock. It parks in front of her home and honks the horn. — Unknown wise woman

Chapter 3

The "Separated" or Still Married Guy

Blah, blah, blah is what you should hear if you happen to meet him. But what he wants you to hear and buy into are the truly timeless Red Flag excuses used by Still Married Guys across the globe:

Still Married Guy Red Flags:

- ☐ "I'm separated and that's basically the same as being divorced."
- ☐ "She or I am in the process of moving out."
- ☐ "I'm going through my divorce and will be single soon."
- ☐ "She's the one that doesn't want to end the relationship."
- ☐ "She's mean to me or doesn't love me anymore."
- ☐ "You might be the one that is going to make me leave because you're so _____." (insert complement here)
- ☐ "I'm doing it for my kids."
- ☐ "I'm doing it for my grandkids."
- ☐ "I don't want to upset my family or mother."
- ☐ "Divorce is against my religion."

The "Separated" Still Married Guy

- ☐ "I'm staying married because I can't afford a divorce."
- ☐ "She's in jail for a long time/life."
- ☐ "She's on life support in a hospital bed and I can't divorce her or I would look like a jerk."
- ☐ "She's mentally ill and lives in the attic."

Basically, it comes down to this. You can do better than to date "separated" still married men. Unfortunately for you, they are a mainstay in online dating and unfortunately for them, they really aren't in any position to date someone like you.

What would it be like to go through a divorce? If he is going through a divorce and you date him for any length of time, this is what you will be doing. Divorce consists of an abundance of negative energy and will take all if not most of your focus and extra time. And it's very likely that he is up to his ears in emotional and financial turmoil.

Is he heart broken and pining after his ex but trying not to let you see it? His closest friends and family will probably call you the rebound. If you really have the need to help someone convalesce, go candy stripe at the hospital. At least there you will be appreciated for your services

Is he talking about how he and his wife – yes, he has one - are spending time apart to date others? Run! You

No Murderers Please!

are a competitor in an event where you don't really understand the rules, you haven't trained sufficiently and your competition has a strong upper hand and head start. You may look shiny and new but at any meaningful level this guy can't see you.

Is there a possibility that a female stalker will enter your life? Or will there be a woman who calls you up, to let you know that Separated Guy is actually married and living at home with her, his wife, and their three children? Of course that's not what he told you.

Responding to Still Married Guy is a mistake in most cases. Leave yourself open to meet someone who's attractive, kind and above all, available.

It's relaxing to go out with my ex-wife because she already knows I'm an idiot. — Warren Thomas

I'm tough, I'm ambitious, and I know exactly what I want. If that makes me a bitch, okay. — Madonna

Chapter 4

The Puppet Master

There is a term in psychology called the 'Dark Triad' which is made up of three personality types: the psychopath/anti-social, the malignant narcissist and the Machiavellian. These are all highly uncooperative, ego driven and disagreeable individuals. They are labeled as a triad because the traits of each often overlap. What makes the psychopath or the Puppet Master different from the other two branches of the Dark Triad, is that he has an extreme lack of empathetic ability that leads to guiltless and remorseless use and abuse of others. You don't want to be a part of this program even if he is the most charming man you've ever met. He is also uniquely considered the human race's only known intra-species predator. Many of the Puppet Master's behaviors may give him an air of being exciting and full of life, but inside there is a darkness, lack of humanity and a complete inability to form emotional attachments.

According to Psychologist Martha Stout, clinical instructor in psychiatry at Harvard Medical School, The Puppet Master may be found in up to 4% of the adult human population and most are not outright criminals or committing murder, although some are. Chances are high that you may know one or may meet one online.

No Murderers Please!

Psychopathy is as common if not more as left handedness in our culture and the numbers are higher in males. Many psychologists go as far as to say psychopathy in the American culture is the number one public health crisis and most people don't talk about it or know how to see it.

One possible reason why The Puppet Master ends up single and online is because their mates have mysteriously disappeared or because not many women want to be around them. The Puppet Master sees you as prey, an object to possess, exploit or possibly destroy, nothing more. His entire existence and being is entirely driven by puppetry—pulling strings to make everyone around him do his bidding. He is not psychotic. He knows exactly what he's doing and what the repercussions may be. The Red Flag list is extensive because the Dark Triad types are often hard to spot and the Puppet Master may be able to stay hidden for years. A top ten list wouldn't be descriptive enough. To really know what you're dealing with, it is necessary to have a lot of knowledge on your side.

Susan L. Brown is a social scientist who has found 'super traits' of temperament that describe the type of women that psychopaths generally target. The women are extroverts and love excitement but are also sentimental. They are able to become deeply bonded to another person. They invest in their romantic relationship and all of their close relationships deeply, either emotionally, spiritually, physically, and financially and in combination. Another interesting trait is they are competitive women who stand their ground, so they are not codependent types. More often than not these women had no abuse as children and so they don't expect to be hurt. They are cooperative, responsible and resourceful. Although, the trait that stands out more than the others is hyper-empathy, and many psychologists and neurological scientists believe this is actually a genetic precondition in people. These traits together make up a pretty amazing woman. And women who usually end up with psychopaths have these traits measuring up to 97% higher than average! So they are highly empathetic, giving, and open but have that part of them where they don't guard themselves because they don't expect to be hurt. They offer up blind trust.

The Puppet Master Red Flags:

- ☐ **Extrovert** - Psychopaths get their energy from being with others. They don't recharge by being alone like an introvert would.
- ☐ **Excitement seeking** - There is an intense attraction at the beginning of the relationship. It seems unusual and more amazing than connections other people have at the beginning of their relationships, more intense. Psychopaths have an electric vibe and seem very alive.

No Murderers Please!

- **Superficial charm** - He's got more charm than most humans.
- **Colorful words** - His use of swear words in texts and emails is generally higher than the average, as are his use of negative or anger words used towards friends, family, coworkers and strangers.
- **Hammer texting** - His texting can be erratic and intense. He may bombard you with numerous texts and then the line may go silent for days.
- **Few first person plurals** - It's not "we" or "us" to him, it's "me", "I" and "mine."
- **Umm** - The Puppet Master is known for disfluencies or to consistently say Umm and Uh more than other people. This is believed to come about from his constant stretching of the truth or his outright lies.
- **Career choices** - He has one of the top Puppet Master careers - CEO, lawyer, media (television/radio), surgeon, salesperson, journalist, police officer, clergy, chef, civil servant.
- **Educated** - The Puppet Master is usually no stranger to classrooms.
- **Uses props** - Don't let this cat influence you with props like a fancy car, nice clothes, a pretty face, a great smile and intense eye contact. He's a vile creature and a master of seduction.

- ☐ **Business man** - Modern business is the perfect environment for him. He goes where his prey is, where it enables him to achieve the things he wants out of life - power, prestige, control, sex, and money. He's not usually found hunting for mice to destroy at a small non-profit or at a cancer research center.
- ☐ **Larger than life** - Does he seem too good to be true? He seems incredibly interested in you. He is exciting and is promising the world with no hesitation.
- ☐ **Sad story** - He may tell you a sad story to see your level of empathy. If you don't come across as too interested his chances of calling you again sharply decline.
- ☐ **Compliments your strength** - He may say appealing things like, "You're the type of woman that would give me the strength I need to excel at my career," or "You give me something to believe in." He throws in false emotion to be more convincing and may even squeeze some salt water out of his tear ducts for added effect.
- ☐ **Street smart** - He automatically and immediately sees your vulnerabilities. He uses this information to try to get you to buy into his world. This tool has been refined and sharpened since childhood.

No Murderers Please!

- ☐ **Kicks the Underdog** - He loves to pick on those he sees as losers.
- ☐ **Rushes** - He may push a relationship very quickly. He wants to make sure he traps you before you see who he is, especially if he sees a highly useful narcissistic supply he can enjoy through you - sex, money, elevated social standing.
- ☐ **Here comes the bride** - Many psychopaths have multiple marriages to their name.
- ☐ **Sleazy** - He's probably got a reputation as a ladies' man among certain circles.
- ☐ **Con** - He is glib, superficial, a fast talker and a flirt. He loves the con. The Puppet Master has great communication skills, charisma and visioning but he is low in productivity. He's an expert in avoiding work but taking the credit for any done. He's especially skilled at getting others to do his dirty work.
- ☐ **Parasite** - He lives off of others in all the varied ways this can be done. He pulls each string to make people move to serve him.
- ☐ **Focused on pleasure and fun** - He's a thrill and a pleasure seeker. He denies himself nothing and enjoys taking physical risks.
- ☐ **Hypomanic** - Imagine yourself after two drinks feeling elated and extremely confident, not a care in the world. He feels like that most of the time.

- ☐ **Irresponsible** - He is impulsive, lacks behavior control, takes no responsibility for any poor actions on his part and lacks long term goals.
- ☐ **Ultra-rational** - Unlike the narcissist, he is not out of touch with reality. He's not psychotic, he's a psychopath. He is generally distinctly rational and goal oriented.
- ☐ **Amoral** – No morals here. Things are good if they get him to where he wants to be and bad if they don't. Basically, this crazy bastard thinks the world and you exist to fulfill his desires no matter how obscene.
- ☐ **Rainbows and unicorns** - Don't cross the Puppet Master or your life may be filled with a series of painful incidents or unfortunate experiences. He may be swift in his punishment or he may wait years.
- ☐ **Achilles heel** - When he can't bring harm to others or cause strife. If you believe you are in the midst of The Puppet Master don't let him see your emotions, especially the good, kind and forgiving ones.
- ☐ **Barely sleeps** - The Puppet Master is bigger than sleep, especially when he's having one of his manic episodes.
- ☐ **Cognitive empathy** - He may display cognitive empathy but does not understand emotional or

affective empathy. In other words, he understands that he's supposed to feel sad for you when your mom is in the hospital, but he is not able to care. He is cold on the inside, but on the outside he's well practiced on appearing normal by years of watching and mimicking others.

- ☐ **History of delinquency** - Was he a law abiding kid or did he give his parents and the cops problems? In his delinquencies The Puppet Master can be quite versatile. His gift probably wasn't just limited to taking out credit cards in his dad's name, physically abusing his grandmother's cat or selling drugs.

To learn more about The Puppet Master, consult the *Hare Psychopathy Checklist* online. Some corporations actually use the Hare checklist to find and hire these destructive humans.

The supply of good women far exceeds that of the men who deserve them.— Robert Graves

Chapter 5

The Mentally Deranged Loose Cannon

Sociopaths or Mentally Deranged Loose Cannons have been considered interchangeable with psychopaths so they currently fit in the Dark Triad as the psychopath/anti-social. They have many of the same character traits as psychopaths but are now starting to be considered quite different from them. You probably won't find too many of The Mentally Deranged Loose Cannons in online dating unless he's a high functioning one and even then, it would probably be rare. Sherlock Holmes calls himself a high functioning sociopath. He would definitely not be one to reach out and try to meet someone online unless for the sole purpose of solving a case. The Red Flags for the sociopath are the same as for The Puppet Master except for the following differences.

The Mentally Deranged Loose Cannon Red Flags:

- ☐ **Crazy eyes** - Will appear to be very disturbed and odd.
- ☐ **No filter** - Not suave and able to hide feelings, thoughts and deeds.

No Murderers Please!

- ☐ **Highly impulsive** - Instant gratification is first on his list of must do's.
- ☐ **Nervous** - Tends to be nervous and easily agitated.
- ☐ **Violent** - Volatile and violent behavior, prone to emotional outbursts and fits of rage.
- ☐ **Could snap and commit an unplanned murder** - His crimes tend to be haphazard, disorganized and spontaneous rather than planned.
- ☐ **Clueless** - Not fully aware of the consequences of his actions due to lack of education and/or skewed world view.
- ☐ **Able to form attachments** - May be able to form an attachment to a particular individual or group, although it is difficult for him.
- ☐ **Doesn't play nice** - No regard for society in general or its rules.
- ☐ **Feelings** - Can feel some remorse or guilt.
- ☐ **Uneducated** - Will generally be uneducated and live on the fringes of society.
- ☐ **Unemployed** - Is unable to hold down a steady job.
- ☐ **Nomadic** - Will not stay in one place for very long.
- ☐ **Skewed morality** - He understands right and wrong but his understanding is off kilter.

The Mentally Deranged Loose Cannon

All men are not slimy warthogs. Some men are silly giraffes, some woebegone puppies, some insecure frogs. But if one is not careful, those slimy warthogs can ruin it for all others. — Cynthia Helmel

Chapter 6

The High Mach

The High Mach believes all virtues including honesty are expendable if deceit, treachery and force would be more efficient. The Machiavellian is the second type I will talk about in the Dark Triad. The High Mach stands out above the others as a pathological liar and as supremely manipulative in his behavior. He doesn't choose to be a master manipulator, he embodies it. He is deceptive, conniving, calculating and detached. He believes that if people allow themselves to be used, then they deserve it. He may sound like a force to be reckoned with but he is small potatoes to women who can see through him.

Red Flags for The High Mach:

- ☐ **He's pathological** - He will lie about the weirdest things. He will lie when there is no apparent reason to lie. He will lie if it gets him where he wants to be or if it gives him power by misinforming you. The problem for him is the bigger the lie, the harder it is to cover, just like his bald spot.

- ☐ **Manipulative** - The High Mach is more deceitful and self-serving than other people. He will never tell anyone the real reason he does anything unless it's useful to him. He is easily entertained by lying to you. It's possible on your first time meeting him he could say something as shocking as that he murdered his father or that his mother is in an asylum.

- ☐ **Has an agenda** - Enjoys playing sinister games with others like 'conceal your intentions', 'get others to do the work for you, but always take the credit', 'make other people come to you — use bait if necessary', and 'learn to keep other people dependent on you'.
- ☐ **Charming** - He will use subtle charm, friendliness and the appearance of self-disclosure to get what he wants and to mask his intentions. If these don't work, he will use guilt, threats or pressure but you may not see this early on if he is a High Mach. He will come across as a nice genuine guy as long as he's getting what he wants.
- ☐ **Driven** - He does not simply wish to become the top in everything, but wishes to do so by climbing over others and leaving his shoe print on their backs.
- ☐ **Lacks ethics** - The High Mach is always aligned with pragmatism and self-betterment, not truth or even a particular set of ethics. He is most concerned with efficiency in gaining ultimate

power and is entirely focused on his own personal well-being.

- [ ] **Cynical** - He doesn't believe people are basically good and kind because he's not.
- [ ] **Respects cunning** - He is cunning and duplicitous and appreciates others who are the same.
- [ ] **Logic scares him** - If you are down to earth, logical and forthright, he will not respect you and will find you boring and weak. Although, logic and fact are an obstruction to the High Mach's motives; they expose him by contradicting his stories with facts. He will be cautious with you if you are logical and knowledgeable. He knows you are less easily duped.
- [ ] **Gets bored easily** - It would be up to you to keep things fresh and creative with this cynical Satan's spawn. Remember, it's about him.
- [ ] **He values people who are considered important** - His motto is that it's better to be important even if you have to be dishonest to become that way. Living a life of honesty and humility is dull and shows naiveté.
- [ ] **He says all the right things** - He will tell you what you want to hear. He uses flattery easily and turns it up to eleven if he feels you are important and powerful.

The High Mach

- ☐ **Watch out for handsome types** - The High Mach is very successful with women and even more so if he is highly charismatic or attractive.
- ☐ **He's confident** - He seems to have good self-esteem.
- ☐ **Wants you to drink** - He will try to get you to drink to take advantage of you.
- ☐ **Doesn't get caught** - He doesn't think being a criminal is a problem, but getting caught is.
- ☐ **Boundaries are imaginary** - He is highly functional in careers and social situations where rules and boundaries are ambiguous, such as running a company or sales.
- ☐ **Controlled** - His impulse control is very good allowing him to be a patient opportunist.
- ☐ **Not into the arts** - He naturally wouldn't spend time reading poetry, visiting an art gallery or studying music to any depth because it's time ill spent.
- ☐ **Sexually deviant and wicked** - He is likely to be more open, promiscuous and hostile in his sexual attitudes. He is also known for his self-serving deceptive tactics, such as cheating and/or telling other people things that are meant to be private.
- ☐ **Plays dirty** - He's the kind of guy you would choose to be on your team if all you cared about

No Murderers Please!

was winning and didn't care who got hurt in the process.

☐ **Small social circle** - Most people if they knew him would not choose him as a friend, colleague or romantic partner so aren't we lucky, he's available and probably online!

☐ **Lacks responsibility** - Nothing is really his fault, how could it be? He's perfect.

☐ **Anxious** - He is generally higher in anxiety and neuroticism and low on conscientiousness and extraversion (Hexaco Personality Inventory).

If you want to look further into your own personality, the *Hexaco Personality Inventory* is an interesting study. It can help you understand yourself better and help you understand if you are a target for this type and/or other egomaniacs.

Every time you don't follow your inner guidance, you feel a loss of energy, loss of power, a sense of spiritual deadness — Shakti Gawain

Chapter 7

The Wolf in Sheep's Clothing

You may need PTSD counseling if you spend too much time with The Wolf. This is not unheard of in women who have spent many months or years with The Wolf and his deep reservoir of hatred. The malignant narcissists complete the cynical characters of the Dark Triad. The occasional axe murderer may sometimes be able to hide his intensions but it's the malignant covert narcissist who is often the most difficult to spot and by most accounts the most emotionally dangerous. His ways are insidious and he will strip you of your self-esteem and your mental peace if you let him. His cruelty is subtle. Covert narcissists or Wolves in Sheep's Clothing, tend to choose a caretaker personality type as a partner.

The term narcissist gets thrown around a lot these days and yes, we all probably have different levels of narcissism that we nurture in our own personalities. There are malignant narcissists who are at a minimum, bat shit crazy, and from there most of us hit the spectrum somewhere on the way down to earth. But finding a man to date who has less than more narcissistic traits and not many more than you possess, is key.

The Wolf is a malignant covert narcissist. Most of this sinister beast's wretched existence is spent hiding his true self. He and his massive ego know that showing who

No Murderers Please!

he is and what his intentions are will inhibit his quest for power, money, sex, admiration, attention and the self-centered success that he lives for. As a narcissist he believes he is superior to all but what makes him different is that The Wolf hides his world view from others. He is an attention monger who seeks it in hidden and subtle ways. He has delusions of grandeur and actually believes that he alone should decide who lives and who dies. He is not completely in touch with reality like The Puppet Master is.

He is incredibly hard to spot online, on the first date and probably for many dates to follow. You may sense that he seems reserved, private and introverted. He's really just a creeper. The reason he is so emotionally dangerous is that he is very good at keeping secrets and lies. He is the type that will come across as Prince Charming or that perfectly nice and normal guy. One very telling sign that you're dealing with The Wolf is that he talks out of both sides of his mouth. He lies to himself and to you.

Again, he's not an easy one to spot quickly or even longer term. That's why I give you an extensive checklist. Not all the characteristics will be present in every Wolf, but if your check list shows more than half, your sanity may soon be compromised.

The Wolf in Sheep's Clothing Red Flags:

- [ ] **Intelligent** - It takes a level of intelligence to be highly manipulative and hidden.
- [ ] **Superficially charming and likable** - Very successful in attracting new partners. He's usually the really likable, great guy or even seems normal on the surface. He is likely to have had more lovers than the average. Watch out, this one can be a Petri dish of disease.
- [ ] **Under the radar** - He seems more modest, shy, quiet, inhibited, shame-prone, and reserved.
- [ ] **Shameful** - He often feels humiliation, cowardice, or a sense of failure to cope successfully with challenges, but he guards these feelings with his life. He lashes out or hides if he feels he may be exposed.
- [ ] **Seems really in to you** - Good morning and good night texts right away, great listener, wants to see you and talk to you daily at first.
- [ ] **Team Player** - Knows very well how to look like a team player at home, school, with friends or at work if it helps him attain the power and attention that he prizes.
- [ ] **Hyper conscious of and calculated in his actions** - He may seem like he's got a bit of OCD and will probably move carefully and methodically when

he is eating, putting on his coat, using a napkin or getting out his wallet.

- [ ] **Tics** - He may have some strange mannerisms that he may not notice he's doing if he gets comfortable with you.
- [ ] **Self-deprecating** - He will joke about how he's not that smart or rich, or how he shouldn't have the job he does—if it's a good one. He may crack jokes that make him look humble. Inside he's anything but. He feels he is not appreciated for how wonderful he is and unbeknownst to you, you probably are not sufficiently giving him the props he desperately needs either.
- [ ] **Too nice** - You may hear him say he's too nice and people (he generally means women) take advantage of how nice, kind, and giving he is.
- [ ] **Cynical** - He will probably be cynical like all Dark Triad men, but The Wolf may play it off with charm and make you laugh about it. Don't let this fool you. He means every toxic word when he says people (women) can't be trusted. He believes this because he can't be trusted.
- [ ] **Stormy relationships** - Talks about how his past relationship was tumultuous or intense. All narcissists tend to create drama and are attracted to it. The healthier you are the less he will be

The Wolf in Sheep's Clothing

attracted to you over time as he sees he can't pull you into his drama and delusions.

- ☐ **Anxious** - He is highly anxious and has difficulty relaxing. He may medicate himself with booze, toking up or use other substances to alter his already off kilter consciousness.
- ☐ **Indulgent** - He is a self-indulgent pleasure seeker - which isn't too hard to spot. His spare time probably isn't spent volunteering and taking his granny grocery shopping. He spends his time focusing on his own gratification, whatever that is. Although, he will volunteer if he feels he needs something more in his life to make him look like the perfect guy.
- ☐ **Jesus** - His mother or father thought or still think he's the second coming.
- ☐ **Fixer of problems** - His friends are often worse off than he is. Having friends who are struggling helps him be a rescuer, a fixer of problems and a man who deeply cares for others. Are his friends in good relationships? Alcoholics? Are they working? Do they have lots of drama in their lives? Do they need fixing? Make sure you find out about his friends, and fast!
- ☐ **Job issues** - He may have a good or even great job but he doesn't really have a passion for his work. His work is probably not altruistic or he may be

No Murderers Please!

"between jobs" and living in his parent's basement.

- ☐ **Entitled** - He is entitled but you may not see it on a first date. Watch how he treats others, servers at restaurants, cab drivers, panhandlers, cashiers. He will not speak to them or acknowledge their existence unless he needs something. They are beneath The Wolf.

- ☐ **Silent looks** - His complete silence after you've told him something personal about yourself or have offered conversation on a topic, is a common way he exerts control. He will not answer a question you've asked or comment on something you've said where most people would offer something back. It comes across as dismissive, rude or just plain weird. He also controls through his lack or use of eye contact which can be easily missed by others, apart from his target.

- ☐ **Lacks clarity** - He is not a truth seeker. He creates his own world and will not have a deep understanding of people, reality and how things actually work. He gets utterly confused, threatened and starts to drown when he's pushed past the shallow end of the pool.

- ☐ **Perfect childhood** - He may tell you that he had a perfect childhood and he says this with a straight face. He's not just being good to his parents. He really thinks you're going to believe his bull.

The Wolf in Sheep's Clothing

- ☐ **Expert liars** - He will lie on the first date and you will probably have no clue, unless he tells you that his parents were perfect. But over time you will see that he will unnecessarily lie about little things. Don't worry, there are bigger things he's lying about too. You're not crazy.

- ☐ **Prone to depression** - He gets depressed because he cannot keep himself engaged or interested in anything or anyone for longer than most four-year olds. You may want to ask him early on if he's ever been depressed. But remember, he's probably going to lie.

- ☐ **He does not understand common humanism** - He's only interested in his own needs. He does not want to be burdened by anyone else who may have needs (See Middle Aged Mr. Perfect). Unless, of course he is in his Rescuer costume and he's driving his friend a short distance to rehab for all to see or hear about.

- ☐ **Inability to form intimate relationships** - Is he a serial dater? Have most of his relationships if not all been short term? Is he over 37 and never been married? Or maybe he was married for a very short time, which doesn't count.

- ☐ **No apology necessary** - He is stubborn and will rarely apologize, unless he wants something from you. He may then apologize but it's not because he's sorry.

- ☐ **Extremely sensitive to criticism** - He will eventually end a budding relationship if you plan on giving him any criticism, even the constructive type. If you do it on the first date, you most likely won't see him again. If you suspect you may be dealing with The Wolf, try it out. The sooner you can toss off the sheep's clothing the better!

- ☐ **Highly materialistic** - He is narrowly focused on money and power but he will play it down. He knows that showing his extreme material vanity is not the way to win friends and influence people.

- ☐ **A victim mentality** - He may be blaming others for his lack of a close relationship - his ex was bi-polar or had anger issues, the one before that was "crazy for real." Don't listen to his drivel. HE made them angry and crazy.

- ☐ **Inability to feel genuine remorse** - If he does feel any, it's for himself and it comes from the depths of his ego, not his heart.

- ☐ **Gas lighting** - You feel like you don't know what The Wolf is thinking or feeling. He will twist or spin, selectively omit or give false information in his favor. His intent will be for you to doubt your own memory, perception, and sanity. Gas lighting would probably not be exhibited on a first date but if you're lucky it will. He may ask you if you worry about your memory, or he will say something and then tell you he never said it. No he doesn't have a bad memory, he's a creepy covert narcissist.

☐ **Has unfulfilled expectations** - He wishes his life was different or says he wishes he wasn't single. The truth is that he needs to be single or at least keep a large distance to hide his highly classified and most important personal secrets. If anyone were to get too close, he may be exposed as being just another human male and his empire would crumble to dust. Although, he isn't entirely conscious of this fear of his.

☐ **A tease** - He not only has an aversion to emotional intimacy but he abhors being physically intimate. Here I have to mention the cerebral, histrionic and somatic covert narcissists as they are slightly different in expression.

Often a *cerebral covert* is actually asexual but may engage in sex to keep his narcissistic supply available. This could be your role if you stick around. But as he gets to know you better, he will be a tease and withhold sex. He is a highly sadistic misogynist. To him you, the female are a parasite and a leech that lives to suck men dry. He is projecting what he is on to you. Sex and intimacy are mutually exclusive to him. The closer he feels the relationship is getting, the more repulsive he will find you physically. He will eventually find another outlet either through fantasy or subversive and dishonest behavior.

The *histrionic and somatic covert* narcissists use their bodies and techniques of seduction to obstruct supply from others. In other words, they are only interested in you as a narcissistic supply and as a way to compete with other men by keeping you and probably other women at the same time, from them.

☐ **Emptiness** - He has as much good, solid energy as a headless window mannequin.

A gentleman is simply a patient wolf. — Lana Turner

Nothing is as good as it seems beforehand.
— George Eliot

Chapter 8

Megalomaniacal Master of the Universe

And last but far from the least prevalent in the Dark Triad is the malignant overt narcissist. Our culture breeds them like fruit flies of the male persuasion. We have become so accustomed to the egomaniac we barely notice he's weird. Of course it becomes more apparent over time as you grow to dislike this corrupt cynic, and yourself for being there. But that means you have to invest time with The Megalomaniacal Master of the Universe, and I want to help you avoid that. Thankfully, many of his actions are easy to spot because his antics are far from subtle.

Overt malignant narcissists are easier to spot than the coverts. The overt externalizes his arrogance by being outwardly demanding and by displaying other blatant Red Flags. He is as corrupt as The Wolf at his core but doesn't hide it nearly as well. The Master of the Universe's confrontational communication style does not go unnoticed, especially once he gets into a position of power.

The Master of the Universe online bio will typically have lots of complements directed towards himself by himself. To look less arrogant he may state that his "friends" see him as intelligent, driven, a leader, romantic, attractive, successful, wise, a nice guy, worldly,

No Murderers Please!

and humble. It may lack words like loyal, trustworthy, down to earth and just a regular guy. He will describe himself to the nines. He will include his education if it may impress people, degrees, social standing and titles at work - CEO, Entrepreneur, Owner, Successful, Founder, VIP, Philanthropist, Money Maker.

He typically includes many photos, anywhere from 6 up or to the maximum allowed on any site or app. This could be as high as 25! The photos will show him in various poses doing various exciting activities. The Master of the Universe and his profile fall under one or more subcategories - gloating, vain, cheesy.

Photos To Watch For:

- ☐ **Showing him driving a pricy car** - That may not necessarily be his. He will show enough of the car for you to notice the leather seat or emblem or he will be modeling it and himself by standing near it.
- ☐ **Exotic vacationing** - If he can afford it you will see photos of how well traveled he is, if not he will post one where he is at a destination wedding in a rented tux.
- ☐ **Boating or sailing** - He will make sure he looks like he could possibly own the boat.
- ☐ **Playing polo** - At least it looks like him. It's all about perception with these men.

Megalomaniacal Master of the Universe

- ☐ **Winner** - He's wearing a medal or holding a trophy he won in some sporting competition. If he's incapable of winning his own awards, he will be standing next to a trophy someone else or a team that he's not on won. This may give you the impression that he's a winner too.
- ☐ **Inspiring** – You may find his motto in his bio "I work hard and play hard" or other quotes about living life to the fullest or how he's following his life's dreams.
- ☐ **Hot to trot** - In his photos he is surrounded by seemingly admiring women and flaunting his body if he's in any kind of shape that slightly surpasses The Michelin Man.
- ☐ **With champagne** - The label will be visible. It will most likely be some highly recognizable, over priced brand like Dom Perignon or Crystal depending on his bank account. Either way, he will most likely be overspending to put on a show. It's also possible that one of his orbiters actually bought it.
- ☐ **On stage** – He's giving a presentation as a leader at work, or he's teaching classes to other clueless men about the art of female seduction or how to con elderly people out of their money.
- ☐ **Useless photos** - There will be photos that are basically the same pose and distance and look the

No Murderers Please!

same. Each has no reason to be there but apparently he looks too good to leave any of them out.

- ☐ **I'm too sexy for my cat** - Selfies of him shooting his face from all angles imaginable, but he still has that same weird, vain, exaggerated smile.
- ☐ **Close - ups** - An extreme close up where you can really drink it all in.
- ☐ **Bathroom bicep selfie** - He also makes sure he gets in the pecs too but most likely he will leave out the chicken legs.
- ☐ **Gym selfie** - Gym or pumping iron selfie with spandex and visor.

By the time you're done with his bio, you don't even need to date him. It's like watching those movie previews where you don't need to see the movie because you've seen the whole terrible thing in three minutes.

In his altered universe, he is The Master and is on a gold plated, diamond studded pedestal. He will expect you to worship him appropriately from dirt level. If he gets the sense that you aren't worshiping him properly, like his other friends/orbiters, there will be damaging consequences to your happiness, health and possibly your dog. If he does have friends or past relationships, they are of the needy and co-dependent persuasion and are merely followers and sidekicks. They feed his ego by making it evident that they are lucky to know him, loan him money, carry his bags and drive him places.

Narcissists both covert and overt, are known to have underlying, secret addictions used to self-soothe, or to emotionally numb out stress and anxiety that they keep hidden from public view. Unfortunately, you may have to date The Master of the Universe for months or even years and be around when he has a lapse of self-control or judgment to find out what he's hiding. But if you're up for it, the fun includes addictions to alcohol, drugs, sex, food, gambling, work, shopping, internet use, and chewing tobacco. He may be blatant in other ways but his secret addictions he tempers in front of others.

Narcissism is a value system. It comes in at different points on a scale or levels within a man and is generally consistent throughout his life. Most people don't change and if they do, it's at very small increments. His narcissistic expression and values are shown by his life choices and intentions. You could look at it as a percentage of time in which he chooses to focus on getting his own needs met and his selfish agendas completed compared to time spent being a decent and heartful human being who sees the bigger picture. It's likely that the narcissist will embody other types listed in this manual, such as The Buzz Kill or even The Puppet Master. The types who are especially unpleasant and uncooperative have a foundation of egotism and fear that permeates their personality. From here they sprout their own expression by the choices they make and the values they hold. Fortunately for us the ego is not as intrinsically strong as the heart and when we know how to spot it, it loses much of its power if not all.

There are numerous Red Flags you will be able to pick up on over the phone or on a first date with the Master of The Universe. If he's more successful and worldly powerful these traits will be more pronounced, as he does not have to defer to many people. In his reality he is used to getting away with being his usual dark, evil but charming self.

The Master Of The Universe Red Flag Checklist:

- ☐ **Me, me me** - He will want to discuss himself with you ad nauseam and will interrupt you or his eyes will glaze over if you speak with an important "Me" anecdote.
- ☐ **Deaf** - At the end of the date or conversation you will notice any words you said were like that tree that falls in the forest and makes no sound, because no one was there to hear it fall.
- ☐ **Liar** - He lies.
- ☐ **Ladder climber** - He will often have a good career or be climbing his particular ladder with ease. He and his species regularly rise to the top of workplace hierarchies owing to their unique

Megalomaniacal Master of the Universe

ability to pull the wool over the eyes of unsuspecting souls. This is due to his desire to secure approval, admiration and power.

- ☐ **Fantasy island** - The Master of the Universe stars in his own fantasy that can have any of the following themes: deserving of or currently possessing immeasurable success, possessing extreme power, unusual and blinding intelligence, box office good looks and deserving of ideal love.
- ☐ **Your boundaries are futile** - Boundaries are made to be broken by the Master of the Universe. If you have them, he will do his best to cross them.
- ☐ **No conscience** - The Master of the Universe really doesn't have a conscience that is anything worth mentioning. Is he glib? Does he tell stories about how ruthless he is at work?
- ☐ **The second coming** - He was likely created by a parent or parents who thought he was the second coming. They may have also told him his entire childhood that he was special compared to other children, just like they were.
- ☐ **Drama** - He may talk about dramatic relationships he's had. Since he's incapable of a respectful relationship, it's likely that drama is the only kind he knows.

No Murderers Please!

- ☐ **Low effort** - He will over promise and under deliver in any myriad of ways.
- ☐ **Elitist** - The Master of the Universe has a belief system where he belongs to an elite group of people. Because he is so special, he can only be understood by, associate with and tolerate what he views as high-status or high profile people.
- ☐ **Name dropper** - He is so well connected Keven Bacon is jealous.
- ☐ **One upper** - Whatever you've done or seen, he's done or seen it better.
- ☐ **Shiny** - If he can afford it or even if he can't, the overt will drive a flashy car, live in a prestigious area and cover his incredible body with style. He will also naturally make it a point to be seen in the "hot spots" and other places of distinction.
- ☐ **Paranoid** - He is ruthless and exploitative in business and personal relationships. Be on the lookout for any paranoia he seems to have of being betrayed by others. He naturally believes others approach the world in the same way he does.
- ☐ **Sensitive to criticism** - He will be overly sensitive to any criticism or threat of being exposed.
- ☐ **Twitter superstar** - If he is on Twitter he is likely to have more followers than most as do many of his friends and acquaintances. This is the part of

Megalomaniacal Master of the Universe

his plan for world domination where he attempts to exert influence over others using online behavior. His twitter posts generally come in erratically one right after the other and then the line goes silent for days.

- [ ] **Workaholic** - Is he married to his job?
- [ ] **His time is precious** - He tends to feel many tasks at home and in life are beneath him. Notice if he seems self-sufficient or if he feels his time is too valuable to do regular life tasks for himself.
- [ ] **Rigid, inflexible thinking** - Anyone with a different approach is personally attacking the Master of the Universe. Disagree with him and see how he handles it.
- [ ] **Can not be wrong** - The Master of the Universe will rarely if ever admit he's wrong, and he will try to prove why he's right at any expense to you or the relationship.
- [ ] **Irresponsible** – He will not accept responsibility for making a mistake, and he is an expert at diverting the blame to others.
- [ ] **He's surrounded by crazy people** - Says his ex's and his ex-business partners or colleagues are crazy, mentally unwell, betrayers and liars.
- [ ] **Badmouths** - He will use character assassination as a tactic to undermine his critics and others who pose a threat. Notice if he badmouths or speaks

No Murderers Please!

poorly of anyone specifically. He may be laying the groundwork for the possibility that you could meet this astute person who is on to him and knows things about him he doesn't want you to find out about.

You can't win as he would rather self-destruct and take you out with him than be the loser. If you find yourself in the presence of this vile creature, a good thing to do is to just keep repeating "Sounds good to me," affirming his worldview and absolving you from any involvement. Then get the heck out of there.

People are like stained-glass windows. They sparkle and shine when the sun is out, but when the darkness sets in, their true beauty is revealed only if there is a light from within.
— Elisabeth Kubler-Ross

Chapter 9

Pining Man

Does he talk about his ex more than anything else or longer than you find remotely interesting? Does his story contain TMI (too much information) and go beyond what he would likely tell an important client or his boss in a normal conversation? Whether he's carrying a torch or he's talking about what he has successfully scored on his divorce decree, this is not a heathy situation to be in. If he makes it through your screening and you agree to meet him but then you realize he might have ex issues, pay attention. Be aware of feelings of extreme boredom, suddenly becoming a pseudo therapist or having to listen to some pointless story about his old relationship. Or maybe overall you have the feeling that you're being subjected to negativity directed towards women in general. Mr. Pining needs to go lick his wounds on his own time.

There is no reason on your first meeting that a man should talk about his ex relationship past the basics, "I was married for ____ years and it didn't work out," or "My last relationship lasted three years." Done. If all he has to talk about is his ex's supposed dark side or how wonderful she is/was, you may want to ask for a Beverly Hills style therapist fee, assume he's picking up the tab and tell him you don't work overtime.

No Murderers Please!

Some men are emotional vampires and for curious reasons feel entitled to throw up all over women they just met. It's as if they have this unspoken rule that assumes any woman in the vicinity exists in that moment purely to listen to them complain, bitch and moan. Why wouldn't you want to be sucked dry by his oversharing about his ex's hormonal issues, her personality traits, lifestyle or even what a horrible mother she is? I can't imagine anything more enjoyable on a date, can you? Seriously, we need to learn from her and avoid this guy. Many of us don't even realize that this happens to us because it's so common place for men to dump their emotional issues on women. We listen to them even though we feel irritated and trapped and wish we were doing something else like getting on the scale after the holidays or doing the Lotus Headstand with Bound Legs yoga pose, underwater.

The Pining Man's Red Flags:

- ☐ **Nice ring** - In his profile he may show photos of himself wearing a wedding ring. It's likely that he's not lived much of a life since his break up and probably has no new photos.
- ☐ **Selfie king** - He has only selfies and/or photos with a woman cropped out in his profile.

- ☐ **Going through the motions** - He may give off the energy that he's not overly excited about meeting you—someone new.
- ☐ **Old shoe** - When he talks to you, he seems overly comfortable, as if he knows you already and has expectations of you. He's likely transferring his old relationship on to you.
- ☐ **Snore** - He talks about his ex for more than one or two sentences or brings her up randomly in conversation.
- ☐ **She was a runway model** - He mentions how attractive his ex was. Not only is this man insecure and wants you to know he can get an attractive woman, he's also pining.
- ☐ **Wants to know about the demise of your last relationship** - He asks you about your past relationship. This most likely isn't because he's interested in it or you, but because he wants to talk about his.
- ☐ **Pen pal** - He seems to be interested in gaining a pen pal or having a virtual relationship.

It's not very often that a woman will unload her dirty laundry or overshare with a man she's just met. Some women will instinctively try to lessen the pain of what a total jerk he's making of himself by also sharing too much or even give the impression that she's siding with

No Murderers Please!

him. Don't go there if you're tempted due to your kind and giving nature. If he's one of these blood sucking vampires, use your planned escape route from this graveyard.

While you're getting ready to fade into the mist you might even find a chance to throw in a:
"Maybe she just didn't like/love you anymore."
"It's highly likely that she doesn't really care what you think."
"Maybe it's YOU that made her crazy."
"Why don't you give her a call?"

Any of these helpful comments usually shut him up allowing you quiet time to put on your coat in peace. Or you could go the more politically correct route and tell him he should find someone to talk to, a professional. But that's not nearly as fun.

I am not soft. It is better to be hard, so that you can know what to do. — Pearl S. Buck

Can you imagine a world without men? No crime and lots of happy, fat women. — Marion Smith

Chapter 10

The Peacock: Is He Really Just Metro?

I'm all for clean fingernails, bathing and breath that smells like a fresh spearmint breeze. Most of us wouldn't say no to the well-known metro, David Beckham, as there is definitely a degree of metro sexuality that is acceptable to many women. But then there's a whole other animal I like to call, The Peacock. This is a man who isn't necessarily in touch with his feminine emotions like empathy and sensitivity towards others but who has the grooming habits that are usually considered the realm of the feminine. He has taken them to an absurd and time-sucking extreme. He is neurotic; it's displayed as a preoccupation with his physical presentation and his neediness to be admired and noticed for it. Depending on the degree of his condition, The Peacock may not be worth the perk of getting to stand next to a man wearing Bruno Magli shoes or getting to share a drink with him while you struggle to tear your gaze from his perfectly waxed eyebrows. I've dated metro more than once at what seemed to me to be a workable degree—in the beginning. Later, it ended up to be much of my time spent waiting for the debutant to make his long awaited debut from the bathroom after he made doubly sure every bow was in place. In an uncomfortable role reversal, The Peacock may want to

No Murderers Please!

discuss on a daily basis a potpourri of life enhancing subjects that you may tire of - wrinkles on his knees, placement of his body hair, excess body fat - real or imaginary - skin blemishes that "might be something serious." For every point higher he hits on the Peacock scale, he seems to score ten times lower on the sexiness and super cool guy scales. He may not be into other men, but he seems more like the woman in a relationship, stealing the thunder from even the most feminine of our species.

The Peacock Red Flags:

- ☐ **Needy** - Does he seem upset if you don't text or email back quickly, sounding needy, pushy and a bit whiny?
- ☐ **Vain** - Did he seem to put a bit more effort into his "angles" in his profile photographs than most men? Men generally think they are more attractive than they are, so even a plain man may be as obsessed with his looks and at times more so than a good looking one.
- ☐ **Affected** - Do his smiles in his profile photos all look the same? This is weird. It also shows that he has probably practiced smiling in the mirror and/or takes a lot of selfies and analyzes them.

The Peacock: Is He Really Just Metro?

- ☐ **You both know he's handsome** - His smile says, "I'm a handsome man. You know it and I know it."
- ☐ **Close-ups** - Does he have a close up of his face? It may be so close that you feel like he's intruding on your personal space right through your screen.
- ☐ **Notice me** - Is he looking for compliments or even comments on his photos or bio?
- ☐ **Body obsessed** - Does he seem overly obsessed with staying in shape and being proportioned? Does he use the word proportioned in conversation?
- ☐ **Primping comes first** - Does he show up late to the date? He may have a good excuse, but he's probably hiding the fact that he got lost in the moment while primping.

But let's say you do decide to meet up with a Peacock who seems masculine and sexy enough for you. Then when you're in front of him, something makes you feel like it's not just a metro you're dealing with. There is another type you want to be well versed in, The Passion Fruit. He's on the down low and is skilled at maintaining public appearances of being straight, but he isn't. Here you may not be entirely sure of your own judgement because he doesn't seem to have any of the stereotypical traits you know about gay men. Although, for some

No Murderers Please!

reason he seems like he might fit in quite well at the weekend getaway party on the ferry to Fire Island, a hot spot in the gay scene. You may have your suspicions about him, but the only way you will know that he's a Passion Fruit, is if he makes a mistake and you catch him. Even more confusing is that he could be attracted to you but he also has a secret male friend or friends that he alone is allowed to know about.

Everyone has a fundamental right to be who he is. Until our world becomes unconditionally accepting of everyone's sexual orientation, some gay men will feel the need to pretend they are straight and date or marry women as a way to prove it to everyone else. Until we live in a society where there is true equality, keep your instincts intact and trust yourself or you may be making new friends in the Straight Spouse Network.

The CDC estimates that about 1.8%, of American men are predominately attracted to men and most are probably dating men. So your chances of going on a date with a closeted gay man are low, but it's not out of the question. Yes, it's a stereotype that gay or bisexual men are effeminate, dress well, attend artistic events or have feminine traits and ways of speaking. They could very easily instead drink beer, burp, swear, tell crude jokes, fix cars, like action movies and do voice overs for the Marlborough Man and still swing for the other team.

The Peacock: Is He Really Just Metro?

Even if you're on top of your game and you think you've got amazing gaydar, it may still be a challenge to identify a highly skilled Passion Fruit. Two of my gay male friends made up a fun game to entertain themselves at boring straight parties. It might help you.

How To Find The Hidden Homo Game

Step #1 - Watch for signs and signals.
Because we are dealing with complex humans, there are no sure ways to win unless your homo is highly stereotypical. Below is a list of stereotypical and non-stereotypical signs. If you're able to check off more than half of the traits, your chances of winning increase tremendously:

- ☐ **He's just not that into you** - He may even ask you out but you will never feel like he's that into you. Unfortunately, if he's attractive, kind, intelligent, has great manners and a good sense of humor, you may be in denial about what you are sensing in him.
- ☐ **Gay bars** - Mentions that he goes to gay bars.
- ☐ **People ask him if he's gay** - He's been called gay and tells you this.
- ☐ **Brags** - Brags about being hit on by men.
- ☐ **Pretty** - He has delicate features.

No Murderers Please!

- ☐ **Squeaky clean** – Has an obsession with grooming and hygiene.
- ☐ **Gay and joyful** - Has an expansive laugh.
- ☐ **Let's down guard** - Gets more effeminate when he drinks.
- ☐ **Clothing** - Could easily pull off canary yellow pants.
- ☐ **Manly** - He could conversely be excessively masculine, may even deny to knowing any fashion brands.
- ☐ **Homophobe** - Mocks gay men.
- ☐ **Experimental** - Tells you about having a random gay experience.
- ☐ **Ladies' man** - Acts like a player.
- ☐ **Vibes on men** - Lights up when the good looking male bartender or server comes over, or you notice his eye contact with another man lasts a second longer than normal, maybe casts a second glance in his direction.
- ☐ **Taking it slow** - He's not looking to rush into anything.
- ☐ **Gay friends** - Has one close or many gay friends that he doesn't know from work.
- ☐ **Choir** - Has been in a choir and even more, he was a tenor.

The Peacock: Is He Really Just Metro?

- ☐ **Shops till he drops** - Loves to shop and can spend hours just browsing.
- ☐ **Book smart in female seduction** - He may own books on how to please women. He's got to read about it because, of course, he has no clue.
- ☐ **Prissy** - He crosses his legs at the knees comfortably when sitting or points his pinky to the sky when drinking, or both and at the same time.
- ☐ **Self-medicates** - Drinking heavily or doing drugs could go along with a lot of types, but it may also be the case here if he is hiding who he really is from the world.
- ☐ **Dead fish eyes** - His eyes seem a bit distanced or dead because he's looking at you, a woman.

If you suspect a Hidden Homo after playing **step #1**, move to **step #2**:

Step #2 - Throw some gay jargon around in your conversation.
Many homosexual men use it with each other on gay dating web sites or in texting. Not all Passion Fruit's know every jargon word so it's best to go through a few. (See Jargon Words below.)

No Murderers Please!

Step #3 - After you've skillfully presented your word, watch carefully.

Does his face twitch? Does he seem to understand what you're saying by laughing or looking suddenly uncomfortable or fidgety? Does he sit up straighter or pull his head back?

Note: You will increase the ease at which you play the game if you practice these words and questions with your friends and neighbors before you get out on the playing field.

Jargon Words:

- Friend of Dorothy's - An expression that secretly indicates one as gay. Derived from the role Judy Garland played in the Wizard of Oz. You can start the game with the phrase, "Are you a friend of Dorothy's?" If he says, "Dorothy who?" notice how quickly he says it, if he seems like he's fishing for more information, or if he is squinting at you in an accusatory manner. If he looks innocently confused, just work Dorothy into the conversation like, "You know, Dorothy, she works up the street from where you work/live, in the neighborhood at that bar, you know that place around the corner and to the right? Oh well, it doesn't matter. Forget I said it." And then

The Peacock: Is He Really Just Metro?

quickly move the conversation on to the menu or to an art piece on the wall behind him.

- ♜ AC DC - "I used to work with this guy who is AC DC." - bisexual. If he looks confused and doesn't seem to know what it means, immediately explain that you meant to say that the guy loved ACDC, the band, and you had a crush on him and that's how you came to appreciate them for the pioneers of heavy metal that they were.

- ♜ Canadian - "I have an ex who had a Canadian." It's actually the term for an uncircumcised penis. If he looks confused, say you meant that he was a Canadian who smuggled cheap cigarettes (weapons, phone chargers, humans, whatever works for you) over the border for your friends.

- ♜ Cake Boy - "My old neighbor was a cake boy." - homosexual man. Obviously here you would say he was a baker who looked really young for his age, and then go into how you loved the margarita cupcakes with tequila buttercream frosting he would bring you for feeding his cat when he had to work late.

- ♜ Flinking – "You seemed to be flinking. (Pause, wait for his reaction, then) Am I boring you?"

No Murderers Please!

Now you have pulled out the big guns and will possibly win the game within seconds. Flinking means to date women to prevent the suspicion of being homosexual. (In urban lingo it means to space out or check out of a situation or conversation). If it's apparent that he understood you, wait for his response. Here it could go either way. He may know the urban term or he may let something slip. This one can be very interesting. I must add that not every gay man will have heard of this term in either sense.

Background Info for understanding your opponent:
Why would a man want to hide his true sexual identity behind a woman?

- Being married to a woman is a useful front. It's still not easy being gay in today's society. There is still a lot of ridicule, discrimination and hatred.
- He is in the military.
- He doesn't want to be gay; it's a difficult life to lead.
- He wishes to have a traditional life.
- He's a "straight gay man" or in the "iron-closet" and will not admit to himself he's gay.
- He or his family might be religious.
- He may fear being rejected by one or both of his parents.

The Peacock: Is He Really Just Metro?

- He is a corporate executive that may need a cover.
- He may have children and doesn't want them to find out.
- He thinks feelings towards men are normal and that everyone hides it.
- He may fear being physically, socially or emotionally harmed.

Every human being has, like Socrates, an attendant spirit: and wise are they who obey its signals. If it does not always tell us what to do, it always cautions us what not to do. — Lydia Maria Child

Chapter 11

Whisky Dick

He may advertise he's a "social drinker." This means any time he's with anyone including you, it's a social event and he's going to drink. It seems that online dating is inundated with drinkers. I see it, other women see it and it perplexes us. It's hard to tell if they need a date because they drink too much or they drink because that's the norm out there. In my book, *Don't Kiss The Frogs,* another in The Red Flag Series, I talk about drinking and how it may not be wise to go past a couple of drinks on a first date. You're usually better off not drinking at all. If you want to weed out the guy who sees himself as a social drinker but is actually more of the functioning alcoholic, it may be tough before the first date. It may even be hard to see what his addictions are the first time you meet him, especially if you also partake in a few wobbly pops yourself.

Most men are not going to advertise that they are practicing alcoholics. Different people have different opinions of what drinking too much is. Some men have a couple of drinks daily which is considered moderate for a man according to The National Institute on Alcohol Abuse and Alcoholism. There are studies that show people who drink moderately live longer and are healthier. While other men might have a couple and

The Whisky Dick

then a whiskey chaser or a few on any given night which moves him into Whisky Dick realm.

For those of you who like to have drinks, studies show that couples who have the same drinking habits tend to have similar lifestyles and that helps relationships last longer. But if you don't have experience with alcoholism, it might be harder for you to notice that he is out of control. For this reason it's helpful to watch his behavior first and foremost but also listen to hints he may give you about his problem.

Alcohol in small amounts can improve a man's erection, increase libido because of its vasodilatory effect and the suppression of anxiety. So when he's had a couple of drinks, his blood swells up along with his penis and his amorous mood. But these benefits belong only to moderate drinkers and their partners. If you are with a Whisky Dick and he's over served himself again as he tends to do, his body is not capable of closing off the vessels efficiently, the crucial function needed to maintain a solid erection. If this isn't important to you then make sure that dating a man who sleeps too much, spends his money on booze, stays out too late, pees in his bed, smells like a brewery and dances aggressively with no respect for other people's space aren't either. Along with a less than satisfying sex life, this Bacchus may bring more unpleasant things into your life. Often the Whisky Dick has physical, mental, relationship and legal problems that he's cultivated from years of over serving

No Murderers Please!

himself. In the end and probably in as soon as a few short months, he will put drinking and any other addictions he has before you without a second, third or fourth thought.

The Whisky Dick Red Flags:

- ☐ **Posing with his Bud** - In his profile photos is he holding up a beer or a drink as if he's saying cheers, it may not mean he's a heavy drinker, but he's advertising his lifestyle, especially if he's holding a Bud Light. Does anyone drink that for the taste? If he's showing alcohol in most of his photos or he is in bars, this is a huge hint. Some men even post a picture of the drink alone in all its beauty.
- ☐ **He's over the moderate limit** - Has more than two drinks on your first date.
- ☐ **Loudmouth soup** - Wants to do shots of strong liquor.
- ☐ **Joint of no return** - Fish around to see if there is a bar that he isn't allowed into because of a past altercation.
- ☐ **May have low capacity for executive control** - His ability to make wise decisions is on the low end of the spectrum. Some scientists believe this is genetic and can be passed on to offspring.

The Whisky Dick

- ☐ **Party guy** - Loves to attend events that are focused on drinking and partying.
- ☐ **Member of the blackout brigade** - His friends are drinkers/partiers. Does he mention any of his close friends as being alcoholics? He spends his time in activities and with people where alcohol is the VIP at the party.
- ☐ **He's got mysterious bruises and cuts on his body** - These are more easily seen when he's wearing clothing for warm weather. He's had an MDA or Mysterious Drinking Accident where he wakes up with bruises and cuts he has no recollection of receiving. These are also called UPI, Unidentified Party Injury or UBB Unidentified Beer Bruise. If you see marks, just ask him about them!
- ☐ **Self-medicates** - His job may be stressful and he seems to use alcohol to take the edge off.
- ☐ **Addictive personality** - Has other addictions - tobacco, gambling, prescription drugs, gaming.
- ☐ **Drinking stories** - Many of his stories are about how he and his friends were drinking and it's all a blur or a DUI after that.
- ☐ **Booze coupons** – What he calls money.
- ☐ **Talks about his ex who drank** - His last relationship may have ended due to her "drinking too much" or he says he hated fighting with his ex

No Murderers Please!

when she was drinking. Basically, his lifestyle involves drinking to a very large degree, from who he is, to who his friends are and who he tends to date.

☐ **Roadside Olympics** - Has he ever had to take a sobriety test?

In Macbeth, the wise Porter told Macduff that drinking: "provokes the desire, but it takes away the performance... it makes him stand to, and not stand to; in conclusion, equivocates him in a sleep, and, giving him the lie, leaves him." — Shakespeare

Chapter 12

Middle Age Mr. Perfect

He's still looking for that perfect woman to match his own perfection. He's not going to "settle" for you or for anyone. At least that's the story he's telling himself. This is the same story that he will be telling you later if you choose to spend time with this confused mess. If he's pushing 40 and has never been married or in a serious committed relationship for many years or has had only a token marriage of some months, he's probably a Mr. Perfect. If you are willing to waste your time entertaining a middle-aged Peter Pan on his island of one, here are some reasons why you may want to build a raft for yourself as soon as you make that questionable decision.

Luckily some sites require a man to list if he's been married and if he has children, so he's easy to spot if he's older. He may tell you up front that he has never been married although he is probably aware by now that some women see a huge Red Flag sticking out of the top of his head when they hear that. He will in most cases, be proud that he's so "picky", or he will act as if he's been spurned by crazy or cheating women. It hasn't been his choice to be single. He will likely have his story planned so that you understand that he is normal.

No Murderers Please!

Mr. Perfect lives on Fantasy Island. He will exaggerate about how close, good or long his past relationships were. In his own mind he thinks he will be in a committed relationship some day with someone who's his perfect mate, his soul mate, but deep down he is just too insecure to accomplish it. He doesn't trust himself and you can be sure, he will never trust you.

Once you get to know Mr. Perfect, he's really pretty odd. Mr. Perfects are extremely reactive to fear that arises from intimacy or, in other words, they are emotional cowards. Mr. Perfect will eventually take the wind out of your sails, the happiness out of your life and if that's not enough, whittle away your self-esteem one sweet day at a time. Many social scientists see these individuals as men who relate to others in a way that allows them to isolate themselves and to keep others at a distance. Mr. Perfect has a triple threat defense system going on: avoidance, isolation and distortion. Even his family members sense these things about him. If Mr. Perfect feels himself getting close to you, his defenses will pop up in all sorts of odd and life-draining ways.

Due to his formidable skills in the art of being able to justify anything to cover deep-seated terrors, Mr. Perfect feels satisfied at a shallow level. He is often self-righteous with his life choices and about being forever single. You could consider the type very imaginative. He spends energy trying to avoid the feelings of angst he has when he is involved in intimate relationships of any sort. He believes that uncomfortable feelings should never exist and if he feels them, the relationship is to blame. He does not know himself well enough to understand that he is simply out of his comfort zone and instead sees them as negative. When Mr. Perfect's defense mechanisms are challenged, he gets extremely uncomfortable and pulls away, isolating himself emotionally. He attempts to distort reality in your mind and in his own by reverting to his Fantasy Island. Everything is safe and makes sense to him there. Some Mr. Perfects may get to a point where they realize at a deeper level that they are not very happy with how their life is turning out, but they don't know how to change. Unless you have codependency issues, this is not your problem.

Other than the fact that he's never been in a truly committed relationship, Mr. Perfect may be difficult to identify until you've wasted months or even years of your life in a one sided love-affair. I suggest seeing the Red Flags available in Middle Aged Mr. Perfect sooner than later.

The Middle Age Mr. Perfect Red Flags:

- ☐ **The favorite uncle** - If you have children, he will think he relates to you by saying he's got nieces and nephews.
- ☐ **He just hasn't found the right woman** - He may think in the back of his mind he will eventually

find his younger and mutually perfect woman to start his family with and THEN live happily ever after in his idyllic world. And it's somehow a given that this younger perfect woman won't mind that he's balding, shallow and stuck in his ways.

- [ ] **Dates younger** - He is trying to date the age he wishes he was. He may show in his profile that he is looking for women who are in a generation that he himself isn't a part of.
- [ ] **Never married** - If he's over 37 and has never been married, chances are very low he will ever commit to anyone, including you.
- [ ] **Puts down or makes fun of marriage** - Not only is he afraid of marriage, he is afraid of any real commitment and responsibility towards another person.
- [ ] **Picky** - He brags about how picky he is, as if the rest of us would be open to picking Bozo The Clown or someone we consider boring and unattractive to spend our time with.
- [ ] **Dramatic and self-absorbed** - He believes his life, work and past relationships are much more intense than pretty much anyone else's.
- [ ] **May not ask many questions about you and your life** - It isn't because he wants things to develop

naturally or doesn't want to seem nosy, it's because he really doesn't care and is keeping his distance.

- [ ] **Trendy** - He often has the hairstyle and clothing of the younger generation that he wants to be a part of. For example, his hair is longer and coifed or falling over his eyes in the front to cover a receding hairline, clothing that looks awkward on him because he's aged past them — both feeble attempts to try to throw the dog off the scent.

- [ ] **Insecure** - He gives off a vibe that seems insecure or a bit socially clueless.

- [ ] **May have posted photos of himself and his dog** - or even worse, just his dog.

- [ ] **Lack of long romantic relationships in his past** - Unfortunately, he will distort this information so it will be difficult to know the real truth early on, if ever. Find out if you have any people in common so you can do some recon. Did he really live with someone, or did she just live across the hall in his building?

- [ ] **Looks out for #1** - He doesn't give the vibe that he would be someone you could ask to be your emergency contact in most situations. He wants to fulfill his needs alone and doesn't want the burden of any you may have.

No Murderers Please!

- ☐ **Passive** - Mr. Perfect will often have an air of complacency, passivity and lack of engagement with you, other humans and in private, probably his dog as well.
- ☐ **Lacks emotion** - He will suppress his real emotions (See Covert Narcissist).
- ☐ **Seems distanced from life** - He does not outwardly react to anxiety-producing events. He probably has a pretty good poker face.
- ☐ **Nomadic** - It's easier to keep your distance if you're moving a lot or traveling for work or pleasure.
- ☐ **Controlling** - He has an unfortunate but resilient penchant to be in control and have things his way at all times. The relationship must always go at his pace. If he asks you what you would like, it's him giving you permission to make the choice (See The Buzz Kill).

The problem with most men is they're assholes. The problem with most women is they put up with those assholes. — Cher

Chapter 13

The Clueless Clown - AKA - "You Think You Have a Chance with Me?" Guy

Most of us at this point, if we are dating, out in the world and functioning as an adult have a pretty good idea of where we stand on the physically attractive scale. But The Clueless Clown has a few of his pages stuck together and is more delusional than most men. Either his mother has been lying to him for years or he sees himself as he was twenty years ago before the comb-over and the beer gut. Some Clueless Clowns are confused about most things. They don't get the look of disgust on a woman's face, the meaning of complete lack of eye contact, or why she went to the bathroom and never came back. I call these Class 2 Clueless Clowns. We will deal with those later.

Rarely will the Class 1 Clueless Clown attempt his moves when anyone is watching. If he does approach a woman in public who is probably way out of his league, there will be genuine awe, bewilderment or pity from the onlookers. Online however, he is much more active. It's easier for him to attempt to talk to a woman he would never walk up to at a bar, under the protection of the online site. The Clueless Clown unlike many of the types, can be considered a relative term. If because his being a founding member of his church's clown group

No Murderers Please!

causes one woman to deem him out of her league, he may be just what another woman finds fascinating. You may encounter what you personally see as a Class 1 Clueless Clown online, but he's pretty easy to weed out by just ignoring and freeing him up for some other lucky lady.

A Class 2 Clueless Clown poses more of a problem as he may look good to you at first. Until your first date you may not be able to figure out that he's living in an alternate universe. Even though The Clueless Clown is a relative term, there are some things that over time will probably make most women contemplate murder or at a minimum, castration.

Clueless Clown 2 Red Flags:

- **Duh** - He's clueless about how he comes across or that he's been friend-zoned.
- **Not all there** - He's easily overwhelmed by life, luggage and responsible outerwear.
- **Letch** - He's clueless about how you feel being looked at as if he's been locked up in a high security prison for a few years.
- **Insulting** - He says things like, "Why can't I find anyone?," when he's sitting there looking at you. There is a myriad of idiocy that can come out of his mouth.

The Clueless Clown

- ☐ **Insensitive and dull** - He's clueless about how you feel about pretty much everything.
- ☐ **God's gift** – He's one of those perfect specimens who comment negatively on how women don't look the same in person when he meets them as they do on the dating site. Whether he's talking about someone else or not, it's just not fun to be around. It's not the woman's fault he can't tell what people look like through photographs.
- ☐ **Zzzz** - He doesn't notice you are bored.
- ☐ **Not charming** - He has no compliments for you, barely smiles, starts off the meal with conversation about his allergy to dust mite fecies.
- ☐ **Attention span of a gnat** - He's checking out other women in the room either actively or on the sly. His eyes may be so busy darting around when he thinks you don't notice that you actually loose your train of thought in a conversation. He hasn't figured out yet that women ALWAYS notice.
- ☐ **Internet addict** - He's randomly checking his phone, emails or Facebook on your date if for some reason you happen to walk away for a few seconds or someone else talks to you. Any chance he gets he's on it.
- ☐ **Bathing is optional** - He smells.
- ☐ **Dental hygiene is optional** - His breath smells.

No Murderers Please!

- ☐ **Nosey, lacks boundaries** – He asks you how online dating is working out for you and other personal questions that are none of his business.
- ☐ **Lives in denial** - He may tell you something to the effect of why his marriage or last relationship ended: "She just left out of the blue. I had no idea it was coming."
- ☐ **Lacks home training** - He lets you pay for his meal even though he asked you out, takes the seat facing the restaurant, chews with his mouth open, corrects your grammar.
- ☐ **Self-absorbed** - He drives away before you even get inside your house at any time of day and especially after dark.
- ☐ **Casanova** - He assumes you are attracted to him and want a good night kiss even though you just met him in person and are far from interested.
- ☐ **High maintenance** - You've had one date and he expects you to call or text him the next day rather than doing it himself. He eventually calls or texts complaining about how you haven't contacted him.
- ☐ **What have you done for him lately** - You barely know him, but he expects you to remember his birthday, every word he said, and give him

whatever else his ego thinks you could do to make him feel better.

☐ **Wants to be pursued** - He plays hard to get to appear more desirable and interesting.

This is the type of guy who really won't notice things didn't go well on your date. He won't notice much that has to do with any social interaction he was involved in. He will continue to text or call to ask you out even if you tell him you would rather drink poison than go out with him again. Don't respond to him because you pity the fool. Don't waste your time or his and just move on.

Ignore him! Some guys are just good at throwing shit at the wall hoping that eventually something will stick. — Dawn Faulkner

I'm dating a woman now who, evidently, is unaware of it.— Garry Shandling

Chapter 14

Mr. You're OK, I'm Not OK

"Damn girl, you're smarter than I am! I'm out of here!" Mr. I'm Not Ok is inhabited by a paranoid loathing for anything that could remotely challenge his sense of supremacy, masculinity or make him acutely feel his weakness. If you have ever been dismissed or disrespected for being intelligent, you were subjected to this man's insecurities. Smart or funny women are not very attractive to Mr. Your OK, I'm Not OK. They make him feel demoralized, weak and useless which crushes his ego more than feelings of being intimidated or threatened would.

Some social science studies suggest that certain men will say they prefer a smart or funny woman and may even believe it, but once they get one live and in front of them they are not so taken with her charms. A study at University at Buffalo of a group of men went something like this: guy says he prefers smart women, guy takes a test, guy finds himself in a room with attractive women, guy is told certain women scored higher than he did on test, guy subconsciously moves his chair closer to the apparently lower scoring females. The study was created to show what people say and what they actually do can be very different in reality.

Mr. You're OK, I'm Not OK

The good thing about Mr. You're OK, I'm Not Ok, is that he will quickly lose interest in you if he feels afraid, less masculine and disheartened because he thinks that you may be too smart for him. He may notice it during your first phone call and if not, he may notice it on your first date. If you're lucky, he will rapidly vaporize into thin air. If he's got a bigger ego and thinks he's pretty smart but can't hold a candle to the likes of you, it may take him awhile to admit to himself that you are, in fact, more intelligent and finally give up.

You may not be able to spot his Red Flags as he will hide his feelings from you and possibly from himself, but here is what to look out for.

Mr. You're Ok, I'm Not Ok Red Flag Checklist:

- ☐ "Huh?"
- ☐ "I don't like being talked to like I'm an idiot" or "I'm not stupid."
- ☐ "How do you know this stuff?"
- ☐ "I'm used to knowing more than most people around me but half the time you are talking, I don't know what you're talking about." He pretends that he's joking, but deep down he's not laughing. He vaguely has the idea that he may not

No Murderers Please!

    be the most astute between the two of you, but he's not quite insightful enough to realize it yet.

- [ ] The two of you have great conversations and he seems attracted but he's holding back.
- [ ] He tries to catch you making mistakes factually, grammatically or other to compensate for his feelings of uselessness.
- [ ] You personally question his abilities.
- [ ] He mentions how you might be book smart but HE's street smart.
- [ ] If you watch closely, when you talk, his eyes may show glimpses of admiration, hatred or fear but for the most part his eyes eventually look glossed over and checked out.

    Mr. I'm Not OK says to his buddies that he would rather have a woman who doesn't challenge him because he is challenged enough at work. He wants to spend his time with a woman who gives him fun and pleasure and boosts his ego. Most truly intelligent men do want to better themselves and do want a woman who challenges them to be better people; they are confident and deeper than the average and they don't belong in this manual. When it comes down to it, couples that generally work better together have closer to equal levels of intelligence, value systems and attractiveness.

Mr. You're OK, I'M not OK will likely hide his insecurities for as long as possible. He often isn't even fully aware of them. Luckily, you don't have to recognize him to protect yourself because he will be the one opting out, conveniently leaving your dance card open for a more intelligent and compatible companion.

I think...therefore, I'm single. — Lizz Winstead, Co-creator Daily Show

Chapter 15

The Buzz Kill

Who's in charge? He's in charge that's who! And if he doesn't get his way beware the wrath of the Buzz Kill. He is a bully who may be tough to spot on dating sites. Although, when you chat with him you may be able to figure him out fairly quickly, giving yourself valuable time to read a good book instead of agreeing on a date. If you're currently suffering from low self-esteem for whatever reason, beware. That situation makes controllers feel right at home. These men don't see themselves as controllers but as simply — right. The Buzz Kill wants to be in a position of absolute authority and power so that you defer to him on all topics. He wants to put you where you belong, idolizing him. Things are going to go his way and because of his seemingly confident, possibly charming and/or convincing manner, he may get away with it for a time.

Many seasoned Buzz Kills are great at hiding the darkness of their personality and behavior abnormalities for extended periods. In extreme cases, psychologists define controlling behavior as a disorder called obsessive compulsive (OCD), where people are rigidly preoccupied with certain things. He may be overly concerned about which way the toilet paper roll faces or how many squares he uses, has abnormal concerns about sticky substances or may be intensely focused on his bald spot or some other physical trait. Above all, he is consistently angling on dominating others at the expense of flexibility, creativity and his and other people's happiness.

There are common traits signaling that you might be in the midst of The Buzz Kill. Use your powers of observation and woman's intuition, and even if you are not at your best, you could see them very early on.

Red Flags For Spotting The Buzz Kill:

- ☐ **Unsolicited advice** - In your screening phone call, notice if he has suggestions for your conversation, your behavior, your availability and your life in general. For example, he tells you that you should be more available to take his calls. If he uses the words "you should" or "you need" in any part of your conversation that is meant to tell you how to behave. Before you send him back to his own planet, you could add a little hint for him to help future females, "I didn't ask your opinion about my life, good bye." If you've never put a random Buzz Kill in place, try it! There really is nothing wrong with forcefully pushing back when you are confronted with aggressive,

No Murderers Please!

disrespectful and egotistical behavior. It feels great!

- ☐ **Mansplains** – Explains something to you in a condescending or patronizing way and may often talk over you.
- ☐ **Stalker** - You texted or emailed him a few times but have never met. Now he's wondering if you're going on a date with someone tonight. The Buzz Kill might also ask you how the site or app is working for you—as if it's any of his business.
- ☐ **Overly critical** - He may seem critical of your profession, interpersonal skills, interests, clothing, parenting, vocabulary or mispronunciation of words or even the restaurant, servers, or food.
- ☐ **Bad sport** - He takes himself very seriously and cannot laugh at himself if it's you making the joke.
- ☐ **Texts** - Good morning or good night texts come too soon. They could happen right after your first date or even creepier, before you meet.
- ☐ **Won't tell you about his inner life** - He seems easily frustrated or angered by what he perceives to be inane questions you're asking about him or his life. Or he may pull out the

charm and evade your questions with humor. He is fully aware that the person who's asking the questions usually has the power.

- [ ] **Angry** - Anger and frustration come easily to him. He may not direct the feelings to you at first but you might sense an underlying anger. His anger might show when he's not able to find his car in the lot, something is wrong with the bill, there are issues with the food, or some topic of conversation isn't quite to his liking. He may also use anger to put you in your place if he finds you guilty of insubordination at any point.

- [ ] **Overly nice** - He may not seem angry. Ingratiating behavior is also a tactic used by The Buzz Kill. Most people have a habit of being nice for casual interaction. When it is conspicuously overdone, it is meant to create a sense of obligation or guilt, and to block confrontation, since that would make you the bad guy if you have any problems with his behavior.

- [ ] **Insults** - The Buzz Kill has a penchant for insulting or putting down women in subtle and not so subtle ways, chipping away at her self-esteem so she is more easily controlled.

No Murderers Please!

- ☐ **Prying** - He expects you to answer rude or personal questions. When you don't answer, he acts as if you have the problem.
- ☐ **Talks too much or too little** - He talks excessively, expecting you to listen and focus on him. Or conversely, he doesn't talk much at all to the point of frustration on your end. Or he speaks quietly where you need to lean into him to hear - also a control tactic.
- ☐ **Points** - Points at you when he's talking. Although, he may point to the floor or lower than your face. He possibly has been told by an ex in the past not to point at her face when he's bossing her around or berating her, so the finger goes elsewhere to avoid a first date confrontation. Either way, let this pique your interest.
- ☐ **Lies** - He lies about something. One lie he often tells is that he had perfect parents or a perfect childhood. (See Overt Narcissist)
- ☐ **Clairvoyant** - He claims to know what you're thinking or seems to think he knows you even though you've just met.
- ☐ **Mr. Moneybags** - He is overly generous with money or gifts. Beware! There are always strings attached.

The Buzz Kill

- ☐ **Projective identification** - Creepy behavior where he will try manipulating you to act in a way that justifies his attitude or position. It usually works this way: An interpersonal accusation is made by The Buzz Kill, which intentionally touches on your sensitivity or pushes a button. It may be directed towards your ability to listen, communicate or understand. For example, he says, "We are having problems communicating." But he means you have them, which you can tell by his delivery and tone of voice. Then if you care enough, you will protest rather than laugh at his absurd, nonsensical comment. If you lose composure, you may counterattack aggressively in a way that seemingly proves his point. He wants you to lose your composure and confidence. He's trying to stimulate fear, anxiety, guilt or shame in you. The Buzz Kill then benefits by gaining the upper hand as well as moving the focus off his issues (See Covert/Overt Narcissist).

- ☐ **Fanatical** - Controllers are also controlling with themselves. They may fanatically count carbs, are clean freaks, are hyper religious, workout fanatics or workaholics.

No Murderers Please!

- ☐ **Deaf** - They don't take no for an answer (see Massage Guy, Overt Narcissist).
- ☐ **Trolling** - The Buzz Kill trolls. He will ask for a general opinion you may have on something. Then he will respond to your answer as if it is a personal attack on him. He draws you into a situation where you are defending your original impersonal statements. If you fall for the troll, you will seem to be actually attacking him. From his point of view, he now has the moral high-ground and hopefully has succeeded in making you feel guilty and eager to do something to make The Buzz Kill happy again.
- ☐ **He loves you** - One of the things that might attract you to a controlling type is how quickly he says, "I love you," or wants to commit to you. The Buzz Kill may give gifts, make promises, and shower you with attention and nice gestures. Who wouldn't be liked being admired so highly?
- ☐ **Just enough** - Mr. Buzz Kill gives you just enough of his time or attention to get what he wants. First, he will not do something he agreed to do. He probably really never intended to do it. For example, he invites you somewhere or says he will meet up with you

on a certain day but cancels, doesn't bring it up again and doesn't follow through or never shows. If you actually give him the chance to redeem himself, he will do some small relatively easy thing in an attempt to make you happy or forgiving. His intention is to make you feel guilty for not being happy, or forgiving. The problem with playing into the behavior is that he will immediately start backsliding. He is working on lowering or even better, completely dropping your expectations as you become desensitized to his non-performance. He does just enough to keep you interested (See The Playa).

Eventually, most of the traits will come to light if you end up dating this toxic man. The relationship will eventually get boring, feel suffocating and lack spontaneity. In other words, it will be a total buzz kill.

Woman's discontent increases in exact proportion to her development. — Elizabeth Cady Stanton

The trouble with women is that they get all excited about nothing...and then marry him! — Cher

Chapter 16

The Playa

The Playa is the supreme expert at giving just enough. He feels you out to see how little he can give you to keep you around. He needs to do this because there are so many other women out there. His motto is, "So many women, so little time." When you are with him, he will give you his undivided attention and make you feel like he's extremely attracted to you. And he probably is. But as soon as you are not in front of him, he's calling, texting or thinking about the next woman, who he is also extremely attracted to. He might be intelligent, interesting or have the capability to go deeper, but his ego will have none of that. He would rather have numerous shallow relationships than one that is deep and meaningful. His ego is telling him that he needs to be The Playa to stay in control and keep the upper hand. This is what he enjoys and what makes him feel masculine, powerful and on top. He's not going to bother with the messy emotional connections that might challenge him in a real way.

There are swarms of men out there that are easy to spot while they are trying too hard to master the art of seduction, but the true Playa is the one that you don't suspect. The Playa is an expert swimmer when it comes to playing at the shallow end of the pool. If you aren't on

The Playa

to him he could keep you wading in the baby pool for years.

He's a fluid character and comes across differently depending on the situation and the woman. He is an expert at personal appearances and self-promotion. The Playa is usually more street smart than book smart, although there are also plenty book smart types that have honed their manipulative skills. He may use his natural charm to take your guard down. This is why he's hard to spot. He is thrilling and comfortable to be around. He's smart, interested in you, and friendly; he has manners and is fun to talk to. Many women quite enjoy these traits. The older he is the more skillful he will be at his vocation. By the time he's in his forties, if he's still choosing shallow over substance, he has probably put in well over the 10,000 hours he needs to be considered a master by K. Anders Ericsson, a Swedish psychologist who is recognized for his research on the acquisition of expert performance. When you meet him, you are getting to experience his life's work. Lucky you!

In online dating, he must first use his charm to entice and to win the chance to meet you. Then he can exploit you. His only goal is to get what his massive ego desires at the expense of his pea sized heart. Depending on his skill level, you may need to spend some time watching a man that you think might be a Playa. Don't take a questionable guy seriously. You won't have to wait long to see the darkness descend because he has the attention span of a fruit fly. Wait him out and keep track

No Murderers Please!

of how fulfilled you feel by his allotment of time and energy towards you. It's likely that you will feel confused within a few months and there may be a vague sense of distrust that you start to feel. Where does he go? What is he doing? What the hell is going on? If The Playa hasn't drowned in a cup of vinegar, the breeze has probably pushed him off into someone else's peaches.

The Playa Red Flags:

- ☐ **Good manners** - He has home training. Without this he could never pull off the shenanigans he does.
- ☐ **Charming** - He is often good looking, has a nice smile and is a good conversationalist.
- ☐ **Doesn't ask, doesn't tell** - He won't ask you questions that might go into the territory of increasing any emotional intimacy between you. He would never ask you if you're dating other people because he doesn't want you to ask him.
- ☐ **He's hot and cold** - He may come on strong and then he may be missing for days.
- ☐ **He's elusive** - Are you confused by his actions? If you have a lot of unanswered questions and don't feel comfortable asking them because you

feel it's not your place, it's a sign that The Playa is in the vicinity.

- [ ] **He's vague** - You can never get a straight solid answer on anything meaningful. He will change the conversation to a funny story to divert your attention, or put his arm around you and tell you how gorgeous you are.

We learn best to listen to our own voices if we are listening at the same time to other women—whose stories, for all our differences, turn out, if we listen well, to be our stories also. — Barbara Deming

If men could menstruate ... clearly, menstruation would become an enviable, boast-worthy, masculine event: Men would brag about how long and how much.... Sanitary supplies would be federally funded and free. Of course, some men would still pay for the prestige of such commercial brands as Paul Newman Tampons, Muhammed Ali's Rope-a-Dope Pads, John Wayne Maxi Pads, and Joe Namath Jock Shields —"For Those Light Bachelor Days." — Gloria Steinem

Chapter 17

The Not Funny Guy

He thinks he's funny but no one else is laughing. Unfortunately for him, most women equate intelligence in men with wit and humor. When we laugh it raises endorphins in our brains and makes us feel good. Humor is also a great way to deal with getting through difficult times in life and in relationships. It's really just more enjoyable to be around a man who sees the humor in life and in himself. For most men, if they've got no game and can't make a woman laugh, they are out of the evolutionary contest.

Women are generally considered not funny compared to males and so we may not be considered as intelligent. But if we look at this from the other side, women must be just as intelligent if not more, to understand all types of humor that is tried out on them. A friend of mine says she doesn't care if a man is funny, but she is the exception. Most of us want a man who can make us laugh. If he can't, he better be fantastic looking, rich or incredibly interesting like an astronaut, private island caretaker or a Hogwarts professor. If he's none of these and you find him to be an annoying little toad, try to resist the pressure of faking your laughs. It's not your job to ease the awkwardness and to make the Not Funny Guy feel good. He's obviously not doing that for you. Not only will you be perpetuating his overconfidence, you will appear to be submitting to him.

Not Funny Guy will no doubt be laughing pretty hard at his own jokes. You could just say "I don't get it," and stare at him with a confused or blank look on your face. There is also a chance that if you do confront him by telling him you don't get it or that you don't find the humor in it, your conversation might actually get more interesting. But if you must smile, keep your mouth closed and don't show any of your pearly whites. In body language showing teeth can be seen as a sign of submission and/or friendliness.

Not Funny Guy Red Flags:

- ☐ **Corny** - Cracks jokes that are corny and may leave very long, awkward pauses where you are supposed to laugh.
- ☐ **You came to see him headline** - He actually tells jokes instead of adding humor to conversation.
- ☐ **Goofy** - Pretends to trip, be a mime, run into things or slip on a banana peel.
- ☐ **Annoying** - Laughs harder than you do at his jokes.
- ☐ **Tactless** - Stories or jokes are too graphic and make you feel nauseous or offended.

No Murderers Please!

- ☐ **Too vague** - Ends the boring and confusing story with "You had to be there."
- ☐ **Doesn't get deadpan** - While trying to deliver dry, deadpan humor, he smiles ear to ear.
- ☐ **Embarrassing** - Starts doing bad impressions.
- ☐ **Uncreative parrot** - Quotes movies or sitcoms.
- ☐ **Crude** - Uses very low-brow innuendos.
- ☐ **Clueless and demeaning** - Says to you, "That was a joke."
- ☐ **One dimensional** - Boring and vanilla.

To circumvent much of the awkwardness, you could protect yourself ahead of time by using the tips in my manual, *The Red Flag Series: Don't Kiss The Frogs*. See the chapter on exit plans. Make sure to block his number to avoid further contact, unless he seems useful for business networking. If that's the case and he asks you out again, tell him you're not looking for a relationship or you would rather date women because they are funnier.

He is a legend in his own mind. — Anonymous

Chapter 18

The Piker

There's a difference between being financially savvy and being a cheapskate. Men who are good with their money don't mind paying for quality and they are careful not to overpay for things. But The Piker doesn't want to pay for quality or for anything for that matter. A man who is completely clueless and cheap will be easy to spot. It's the cheap man with home training rudimentary manners who is a bit harder to see especially if you find him on a going Dutch-dating site.

The Piker would buy you coffee as a birthday gift. He will probably never splurge on flowers or any gift he's not required to give, and even then it may never happen. He may even re-gift to you if he doesn't want something - an old sweater, coffee mug or some other piece of crap in his house he doesn't want taking up space in the back of his closet.

We all have our "love language." Some people give gifts, others time and others use physical touch and affection to show love. Some are always ready with nice words and compliments. The Piker will say he's a time giver or any other type of giver except a gift giver. But as it goes he won't give you anything sufficiently, including his time. It's not that he's not a gift giver, he's just—The Piker.

No Murderers Please!

He may be hard to notice at first because he may actually be picking up the check. It might be due to his view of dating, his generation or even his home training. Eventually if you stick around, you will see that he will spend money on you only when he benefits as well. He might spend money on trips so he doesn't have to travel alone. He'll buy drinks because he doesn't want to drink alone. He'll spring for meals because he would rather eat with someone else than himself again. He'll pay for cab rides because he needs to get to these places too.

And it doesn't stop at spending money. Men who are cheap are often selfish in other ways. The Piker looks at life with a sense of lack that permeates everything in his life. He feels that he doesn't have enough of anything for himself, and he protects what he does have, like a dog that will bite your hand if you reach for his bone.

The Piker Red Flag First Date Check List:

- ☐ **Coffee date** - Asks you to coffee and not lunch, dinner or drinks.
- ☐ **Bad tipper** - Tips less than ten percent or not at all.
- ☐ **Coupon clipper** - He pays for your first date with a coupon.
- ☐ **Complains about money** - Complains about the cost of things on the menu.

The Piker

- ☐ **He's broke** - Talks generally about how he has no money even if it's obvious he is pretty comfortable.
- ☐ **Goes Dutch or lets you pay** - Even though he invited you.
- ☐ **Dry me out** - Skips pre-dinner drinks and/or doesn't offer to get you a drink at any point.
- ☐ **Has a rubber roach in his pocket** - Tries to find something wrong with his meal to get a price break.
- ☐ **Isn't hungry** - Eats or drinks at home before your date.
- ☐ **Loves freebies** - Takes you on "freebie" dates where he doesn't have to shell anything out.
- ☐ **You're the host** - Has you pick him up because he's closer to the venue and then he lets you pay for parking.
- ☐ **Missing wallet** - Forgets his wallet and doesn't seem embarrassed about it.
- ☐ **Forgetful** - Borrows money and forgets to pay you back or makes you have to ask him for it.

The Piker is really not much fun to date or to have a relationship with if you are not of the same mindset. If you give him the opportunity, he will eventually make you feel undervalued and taken for granted. Even if he

No Murderers Please!

does have some extra money, he's going to suck the fun out of anything the two of you could do with it.

If I saw YOU walk in the door, I would have kept that two for the price of one coupon in my pocket.
—Jennifer Lee

Acknowledgements

I wish you
good luck,
good fortune
and
good timing
in your search!

Stevie Striker

No Murderers Please!

Acknowledgements

If The Red Flag Series is entertaining and fun, if it's accurate and enlightening, it is due to a large extent from contributions from these most helpful and amiable humans.

I want to bow to Daniela Miranda for her fantastic proofreading, street smarts and fortitude with my endless questions. I send my thanks to the gifted Dawn Faulkner for sharing her time, her incredible wit and for providing hilarious quotes. Sam Olbekson, thank you for your tremendous computer skills, agreeing to assist me at odd hours with great humor, quality teaching and for being evidence that decent men do exist. A bear hug to Kelli Duffy for her quick wit, brilliant ideas and margaritas, and to Jennifer Lee for her insight, kindness and for being Jen. Peter Savely, thank you for being endlessly patient with my inane questions. I want to thank you for your nonjudgmental analysis and honesty. I must thank Karen Darling for her expert advice, humor and generosity and Simon Goodship for his design expertise and for just being his charming self. Thanks to Kendall Gill for his keen insight and honesty. Special thanks must go to the miraculous Dr. Laura Hussein for her knowledge and thoughtfulness. To my grandmother, Lillian Baller, for her support and laughs. An endless hug to my wildly beautiful, insightful and witty daughter,

Acknowledgements

Mia, who is wise beyond her years, for sitting next to me quietly reading and doing her homework, while I wrote for hours and rewrote for more. To my editor, the gifted writer, Barbara Torba, thank you endlessly for your patience and unflagging enthusiasm and to Steven Torba for his humor and constant support. And finally, my most sincere gratitude to Scott Muller for letting me use his handsome image in that stylish tie.

Bibliography

CHAPTER 2: SPOILED RICH GUY

Joris Lammers, Janka I. Stoker, Jennifer Jordan, Monique Pollmann, and Diederik A. Stapel. "Power increases infidelity among men and women." *Psychological science* September 2011 22: 1191-1197, first published on July 19, 2011.

CHAPTER 4: THE PUPPET MASTER

Jakobwitz, Sharon, Egan, Vincent. "The dark triad and normal personality traits." *Personality and individual differences* Volume 40, Issue 2, January 2006.

Hare, Robert.D. *Psychopathy: Theory and Research.* Wyley: New York, NY, 1970.

Hare, Robert D. *Without Conscience: The Disturbing World of the Psychopaths Among Us.* Guilford Publications, Inc: New York, NY, 1993.

Meloy, Reid. *The Psychopathic Mind.* Aronson, Inc: Northvale, NJ, 1988.

Stout, Martha. *The Sociopath Next Door.* New York, NY: Harmony Publishing Group, 2006.

William McCord, McCord, Joan. *The Psychopath: An Essay on the Criminal Mind.* Princeton, NJ: Van Nostrand, 1964.

CHAPTER 5: THE MENTALLY DERANGED LOOSE CANNON

Goldman, H.; Lindner, L. A.; Dinitz, S.; Allen, H. E. "The simple sociopath: Physiologic and sociologic characteristics." *Biological psychiatry* Vol 3(1), 1971.

Porter, Lynette. *Sherlock holmes for the 21st century: Essays on new adaptations.* McFarland & Company, Inc. Jefferson, North Carolina, 2012.

Stout. Martha. *The Sociopath Next Door.* New York, NY: Harmony Publishing Group, 2006.

CHAPTER 6: THE HIGH MACH

Dreber, Anna, Johannesson, Magnus. "Gender differences in deception." *Economics letters* 99.1, 2008.

Ramanaiah, Nerella V, Byravan, Anupama, Detwiler, Fred R.J. "Revised neo personality inventory profiles of machiavellian and non-machiavellian people." *Psychological reports* Volume 75, Issue,1994.

No Murderers Please!

Turner, Charles F., and Daniel C. Martinez. "Socioeconomic achievement and the machiavellian personality." *Sociometry* 40.4, 1977.

CHAPTER 7: A WOLF IN SHEEP'S CLOTHING

Chapman, Gary. *The 5 Languages: the Secret to Love that Lasts*. Northfield Publishing; Chicago, IL, 1st Edition, 2015.

Goldner-Vukov, Mila, and Laurie Jo Moore. "Malignant narcissism: From fairy tales to harsh reality." *Psychiatria danubian* 22.3, 2010.

Peck, Scott M. *People of the Lie: The Hope for Healing Human Evil*. Touchstone: New York, NY, 1998.

Schuckit, Marc A. "Alcoholism and sociopathy: Diagnostic confusion." *Quarterly journal of studies on alcohol* Vol 34(1, Pt. A), March, 1973.

CHAPTER 8: THE MEGALOMANIACAL MASTER OF THE UNIVERSE

Baumeister, Roy F., Laura Smart, and Joseph M. Boden. "Relation of threatened egotism to violence and aggression: The dark side of high self-esteem." *Psychological review* 103.1, 1996.

Holtzmana, Nicholas S., Vazirea, Simine, Mehl, Matthias R. "Sounds like a narcissist: Behavioral manifestations of narcissism in everyday life." *Journal of research in personality* Volume 44, Issue 4, August, 2010.

Levy, K. N. "Subtypes, Dimensions, levels, and mental states in narcissism and narcissistic personality disorder." *Journal of clinical psychology* 2012.

Summer, Chris, Byers, Alison, Boochever, Rachel, Park, Gregory J. "Predicting dark triad personality traits from twitter usage and a linguistic analysis of tweets." 11th International Conference on Machine Learning and Applications 2012.

Stark, Evan. *Coercive Control: How Men Entrap Women in Personal Life. (Interpersonal Violence)* Oxford University Press, 2007.

Vazirea, Simine, Naumann, Laura P., Rentfrowc, Peter J., Gosling, Samuel D. "Portrait of a narcissist: Manifestations of narcissism in physical appearance." *Journal of research in personality* Volume 42, Issue 6, December, 2008.

CHAPTER 10: THE PEACOCK: IS HE REALLY JUST METRO?

No Murderers Please!

Black, Dan, et al. "Demographics of the gay and lesbian population in the United States: Evidence from available systematic data sources." *Demography* 37.2, 2000.

Buxton, Amity P. "A family matter: When a spouse comes out as gay, lesbian, or bisexual." *Journal of GLBT family studies* 1.2, 2005.

Buxton, Amity P. "Healing an invisible minority: How the straight spouse network has become the prime source of support for those in mixed-orientation marriages." *Journal of GLBT family studies* 2.3-4, 2006

Gaudio, Rudolf P. "Sounding gay: Pitch properties in the speech of gay and straight men." *American speech* 69.1, 1994.

Partridge, Eric. *The new partridge dictionary of slang and unconventional english.* JZ:Vol. 2. Taylor & Francis, 2006.

Rodgers, Bruce. *Gay Talk: A (Sometimes Outrageous) Dictionary of Gay Slang.* Paragon Books, 1979.

Ward, Brian W., et al. "Sexual orientation and health among US adults: National health interview survey, 2013." *National health statistical report* 77.77, 2014.

CHAPTER 11: WHISKY DICK

Gordis, Enoch. "The National Institute on alcohol abuse and alcoholism: Past accomplishments and future goals." *Alcohol research and health* 19.1, 1995.

CHAPTER 12: MIDDLE AGED MR PERFECT

Bartholomew, Kim. "Avoidance of intimacy: An attachment perspective." *Journal of social and personal relationships* 7.2, 1990.

Forsyth, Craig J., and Elaine L. Johnson. "A sociological view of the never married." *International journal of sociology of the family* 1995.

CHAPTER 14: MR. YOU'RE OK, I'M NOT OK

Park, Lora E., Ariana F. Young, and Paul W. Eastwick. "(Psychological) Distance makes the heart grow fonder effects of psychological distance and relative intelligence on men's attraction to women." *Personality and social psychology* bulletin, 2015.

Wilbur, Christopher J., Campbell, Lorne. "Humor in romantic contexts: Do men participate and women evaluate?" *Personality and social psychology bulletin* 2011.

No Murderers Please!

Bursten, Ben. "Some narcissistic personality types." *The International journal of psycho-analysis* 54, 1973.

Buss, David M. "Manipulation in close relationships: Five personality factors in interactional context." *Journal of personality* 60.2, 1992.

CHAPTER 16: THE PLAYA

Ericsson, K. Anders, Krampe, Ralf, Tesch-Romer, Clemens. "The role of deliberate practice in the acquisition of expert performance." *American psychological association, Inc.* 100, No. 3, 363-406, 1993.

CHAPTER 17: THE NOT FUNNY GUY

Bressler, Eric R., Martin, Rod A., Balshine, Signal. "Production and appreciation of humor as sexually selected traits." *Evolution and human behavior* 27.2, 2006.

Greengross, Gil, Miller, Geoffrey. "Humor ability reveals intelligence, predicts mating success, and is higher in males." *Intelligence* 39.4, 2011.

Made in the USA
Monee, IL
10 October 2021